Arctic Rescue

Published by Sapere Books.

20 Windermere Drive, Leeds, England, LS17 7UZ,
United Kingdom

saperebooks.com

ISBN: 978-1-80055-007-0.

Arctic Rescue

Ronald Healiss

SAPERE
BOOKS

Table of Contents

1

IT was just after dawn when Action Stations sounded, and it came like a kick in the navel. You see, I was in the middle of a lovely dream... this same dream I never wanted to wake from, and which had warmed me in the private hours of the night all the way back from the Indian Ocean...

Peg's sweet breath is on my lips, her fingers touching my cheeks, her eyes so very bright. With more force than I mean to use — that's how it always is with me — I pull her to me, clumsily shoving the little gunmetal ring into her hand as I grope for words to go with it... words to last us maybe three years until we meet and touch and kiss again, and I am finished with the sweating seas and the stink of Aden and Alex.

Waking... dreaming

Waking... dreaming... My heart is pounding, pounding until I wake to know it is keeping time with the syncopation of that bleating bugle, and it is not Peg's warm body but the heat of my own sweaty palms, nails clenched in, as the horn brays on: "*Action Stations. All hands to Action Stations...*"

There are 115 men on our mess-deck, the ports are shut, the deadlights down, and it is fetid with the stink of night, a night now broken in a welter of swinging arms and legs, each of us rolling from our hammocks, gripping the cleats as we steady ourselves from sleep and gaze half fearfully one to the other in the dim yellow gleam of the deck lights.

Ginger McColl, the burly red-head, gunlayer on P.5, near me when he isn't flunking for Jimmie the One, thumps me — but I'm not asleep now.

I'm still looking at that kid Thompson in the next hammock, the young Irisher with the features of a slim girl and eyes like green diamonds, who is muttering to himself:

"Merciful Jaesus, Jaesus God…"

"For Christ's sake shut your prayers," yells Ginger, "and get your bloody seaboots on. This is it. The war's started, sonny…"

Somewhere down there, among the flying mattresses and the bundles of clothes, lit with a crisscross pattern under the wire mesh of the deck lights, are my seaboot stockings, and I fight through the pile because I'm not going out to that ruddy gun and catch my death of cold.

Jock Clark, the Padre's flunk, catches my glance as he pushes his long, ape-like arms into his sweater, talking through the neck of it as he does so. "Funny, isn't it, Tubby? Funny when it really starts, I mean."

"Did you think Hitler was going to send us a postcard first?"

"No, but those Nazi perishers are grousing at having to start before breakfast, just like us. Me, I'd feel better if I had a fannyful of kye."

"For god's sake get that Mangaroo out," calls Bill Hutchings. "There'll be hell if Sarge sees him; if Sarge is awake now…"

For one minute I, too, think the young Irisher is asleep in his hammock, but as I pull the blanket off the kid Thompson — the one we call Mangaroo because of his angular, flaying legs like a young kangaroo — he strikes out with a sullen: "Leave me be. I'm getting out."

And then I can see what he was doing — tucking a crumpled photo in his belt. And I feel kind of ashamed.

"Put a nick in it, kid," I say quietly. "We've got to get to that gun damn quick. If you're feeling like lumping projjies, that is."

"You've got a bigger belly for it, Tubby," he grins, with those wide diamond-green eyes, and I kick his rump to help him on his way off the mess-deck.

And then we all go stumbling and scuffling after him, Jerry Rotherby, the Surgeon-Commander's flunkey and my rammer-hand on the gun; Ginger Woollon; that big, gangling Taff Evanson; Mickie Bolan, the other Irisher in our gang, and all the other characters in this dim-lit, grey-steel posser world which has been the life of all the hundred-and-more Marines like me ever since *Glorious* was commissioned. And we've been half-way round the world with her; traipsing the Indian Ocean, Suez, the Red Sea, back around Greece and Crete, looking for the war that Dönitz bragged about but which doesn't exist, not out there anyway.

The echo of running feet dies away and our part of the henhouse is deserted, and quiet, too, save for the dull roar of the fans as they drive a shaft of air through the low-roofed vents, leaving the blackout blinds swaying like theatre curtains on a first night when the show is just going to start.

For one moment I halt in our mad skelter down the ladders, because I meant to stop at my locker, 83, and grab a couple of photos I keep in there; but suddenly it seems so damn silly, because the pictures will still be there when I get back... I can hear the Marine Sergeant of Flunks cursing us, cursing the Hun, cursing the bo'sun still yelling Action Stations.

And then I remember. My belt. Oh, goddam, I've forgotten my lifebelt. During Action Stations everyone is supposed to wear a belt. I always feel this is a silly sweat, and keep my belt half inflated in my locker. What the hell's the good of a belt anyway? You couldn't float, with your tin helmet, seaboots and dufflecoat. Or maybe you can. Maybe I'll find out. Maybe I'm fat enough to float anyway. Maybe the sergeant's forgotten his own belt in the panic, and I begin figuring if he'll have the guts to put me on a charge if he can't find his belt either.

By the time I've figured this out, I've reached the gun.

The gun.

Two and a half years of my life with the *Glorious* have been round that gun, when I'm not flunking for the officers, and I love that gun like my own two arms. The *Glorious*, flat-topped old barmaid, is a carrier for aircraft, and they're all right. Gladiators, and Skuas, and Swordfish, yes, they're all right. But it's guns that will win this war. Maybe our gun will win it.

Gun P.7. The gun who runs our gun-crew. There are Bofors in the quarterdeck gun-position P.8, but our gun is a four-point-seven like all the rest port and starboard. Marines man P.5, 6, 7 and 8. The rest are manned by matelots. There are gun positions S.1 to S.8 on the starboard side just the same, but I've never wanted to man any other gun but P.7, and P.7 knows it. She's part of our team, the same crew we've had all the commission. P.7's a grand old girl.

P.7 is in a bay in the carrier's flank, like the others; then there are two blank bays for boats or ammo lockers; then another gun-bay; and that's how it is all the way along. All the bays are open to the sea, with only a rubber-covered girder as your upper horizon to fix the limits of shooting, or you'd hit the flight-deck.

Our P.7 crew consists of the layer, trainer, rammer, sight-setter, first and second fuse-setters, and two ammo supplies to hump the projjies from the trollies to the post. The gun, like us, is only human. She's a bitch who has to be coaxed and fed, and who blasts the living daylight out of you at the consummation of her fire.

No wonder I love that gun.

The chaps, hooded in their duffle llamis, are standing quiet and awkward, because this isn't just a practice shoot, like all the others for two years gone. It's the real thing at last, only none of us knows what the real thing is going to be like.

Glorious is shuddering with speed, flinging spray back over her nose, and because we feel a lot of bloody fools standing there just looking at each other, we turn and gaze out to sea, out over the sharp-cut wheel of the horizon where there ought to be a target. But if there is we can't see it, and with the war so new we don't know what target we're looking for anyway.

Jerry Rotherby, eyes squinting, wonders if he can see better than the lookout, and voices the thoughts of all of us: "He's looking after his ruddy self. Felt lonely up there, maybe, and thought he saw a seagull…"

"Ruddy fine time to be seeing seagulls. Must be just after dawn."

We're in northern waters, and it never really gets dark. You can't tell for certain what time it is. But it is just the hour when a lone reckie plane might be coming down from Vaagso or Maaloy Island way, the dim sea light making a good cover for just one aircraft taking advantage of the chain of cloud cover over the Indreled, that narrow passage which stretches along so much of the Norwegian coast. And after the lone spotter, perhaps a wave of trouble?

We shift uncertainly, odd, cold figures staring into the young sun, and Taff Evanson, the Commander's flunk, ruminates in that quiet way of all Welshmen who like an argument — not a punching row, but a debate all nice and quiet like: "Now, it is not for me to be questioning the movements of this floating fortress, mind you, but if that bastard on the bridge doesn't know what he wants us out here for, well neither do I, and that goes for the two of us. I always maintain they get us out of the henhouse just for the pleasure of it, mind you."

One mute figure cuts the silence as, hand on the gun-switch, he turns and gestures that the first order is coming through. This is it.

I grope for my fuse-spanner, symbol of power. Jerry Rotherby used to be the fuse-setter during the early part of the commission, but then we changed. Jerry is quicker on the rammer, and the lads used to say my belly got in the way. But I liked fuse-setting, and by the time we were at Alex I knew it was the job for me in this gun-crew. It gives you a sense of being needed.

Any fool can handle the projjies or shove in a rammer, but when you set the shell fuses it gives you a feeling of really doing something when you see your shells near the target. You begin to feel as if you're achieving a bit of responsibility.

But until this moment it had never been responsibility in anything more than a practice shoot.

"Projjies... projjies, come on lads. Get those bloody projectiles moving. Check the ready-use locker."

Mangaroo flings back the steel cover. Ready-use ammunition. A locker close to each gun position. So many nose-fused. So many armour-piercing projjies. So many star-shells. Should be about ten or twelve rounds in that locker. Should be. Unless some silly perisher didn't check last time, or P.6 swiped some...

I tuck the fuse-spanner in my belt, swivel forward my fuse-tray, on which the projectiles one by one will be lumped so that first and second fuse-setter can adjust each for range before it goes up the spout. Ginger Dully's my second fuse-setter.

"The fuse-tray's moving, Tubby," Ginger grumbles. "Did you put the pin in?"

I didn't. A hundred, maybe a thousand times I've swivelled that tray out from the gun-foot platform and jammed the pin in, and the drill is automatic. But now I've forgotten to do it, and I know I'm uneasy and on edge; like most of the rest of us, I guess. I say nothing, but stoop, grab the pin on its anchor chain, and peg the fuse-tray fixed. Dully nods at me without a word.

If it is as silent as it was two minutes ago, it is not the sort of silence we hear any more. We can hear the tin-plate rattle of voices through distant Tannoy, and the eardrum rattle of mechanical voices in the earphones, as the orders begin coming through from T.S.

"Looks like it's just a single recce plane," says McColl the layer without raising his head, eyes fixed on his red and black dial pointers. "It's my guess we'll never hit one of those things on instrument firing, even if our gun's bearing. I'd like to have local-fire on the bastard for just ten seconds..."

"Count me out," says Jock. "You boys get your tanner a day extra, and as far as I'm concerned you can kiss the blamed gun right on its tompkin. I want to get back to me hammock."

"Count me out anyway," cuts in Bill. "This is much too early in the morning for me. I'm no good till I've had a shampoo."

Ginger McColl is tense. "For Christ's sake shut that nattering. T.S. is on."

14

There are four T.S. stations, one for each battery. Ours is above the Marine mess-deck, and all the time we're firing on instruments. T.S. are the boys who give the orders and work out the figures. I never did like working out figures. I like responsibility, and that's why I'm trembling, fingers eager to be screwing those nose-cap fuses to right range.

T.S. get their orders from the bridge, where Lieut.-Commander Wells is the gunnery officer in charge, and if T.S. don't pucker up those orders maybe we'll blast this dawn reconnaissance aircraft out of the skies. Maybe.

"Looks like T.S. is struck dumb all of a sudden," says Ginger McColl with a grin. The grin eases from his lips, and the next few seconds become a welter of violence.

"*Fuse to 5,000 yards*," barks T.S. station in my earphones, and I grab my fuse-spanner, lock it in the two ridges in the nose-cap fuse and swing it, rocking it momentarily back and forth as you rock the top of a pepper-mill. "*Fuse to 5,000 yards.*" Fuse 050. Dully, behind me, sets his first projjie to 05 and a half...

"*Fuse to 4,500...*" There is a clank of metal as we re-fuse.

"*Stand by for firing...*"

As Jerry sweats on his first load at the loading-tray, I know why I'm glad I took up fuse-setting. The loading-tray is right up to your eyebrows, and God didn't give men muscles up to there, but, all the same, with the practised skill of a rammer who has fed the gun he loves on every practice shoot for two years, he gets the projjie into place, guiding the nose fuse with one hand while he bangs on the power-ram lever with the other, all in one simultaneous movement.

Tray back. Breech-block back. Ready for firing — automatic firing now we're on remote control.

The majesty — the sheer bloody majesty — of that noise!

It cracks your eardrums and the smoke swirls around the gun platform. The recoil comes out. As it goes past the breech-work, a long arm comes out, swings open the block and takes out the red-hot relic.

"*Fuse* 040... 04 *and a half...*"

Something's moving in on us pretty darned quick, but now we've begun firing a few rounds we feel better. It's that waiting which hurts.

You seldom see anything as pretty as gunfire, especially when it's a clear morning and you can watch the whole length of a shell's flight until it bursts in a plume of purple smoke. In with the rammer. Up the spout. Then we stand tense as the layer swings his handles like a crazy mangle, and black pointer follows red in a wild and waving pattern.

There's a thirty-knot wind which the speed of *Glorious'* passage is flooding back down the flight-deck and curling over to our gun-position three decks below on the port side; and this wind — now seeming like a gale when the guns are bellowing — kills our words. I find myself pressing the phones to my ears, then as a momentary gap comes, I lean over the guard-wires and peer out, over the troughs of tumbling brine and out to the dim-lit morning sky.

"Enemy in sight," rattles the metal voice of T.S. over the earphones, and all eyes start looking for the target. No, not all. Trainer is staring at his pointers. If that bloody aircraft comes right over the ship, we'll have to bring our fuses down 050... 030... 020...

"Local fire..."

The glorious moment we've been waiting for. On the wheel that the layer turns is the trigger for firing, when T.S. have switched us over from remote control. Squeeze that trigger. Squeeze that Hun aircraft out of the sky. Squeeze it hard, boy. And again P.7 gives a billowing violence of sound. As the roar begins to fade, the echo is taken up with the ugly rattle of the multiple pom-poms.

Then silence, broken only by spews of spray on the gently heaving deck. We wait — that fretful waiting. Well, at least we had a crack at it.

Taff says: "You look pleased, man, and I don't mean with your breakfast!"

There is the rest of a bar of chocolate in the pocket of my llami, I remember, and I grope for it and share it round. We wait. We go on waiting.

After what seems an eternity, Jerry points and we all look up. "It's nice being on the busy side," he says quietly. What he means is we are on the port side, and though lower than the flight-deck, we can see what is going on, as aircraft usually take off and bank on the port not on the bridge side. We can see a figure up there adjusting his helmet strap, and there is a little cluster of men — aircraft handlers, they are — waiting on the sponsons below the flight-deck itself. The drumming roar of a Gladiator revving up reaches us, down here on P.7, like a muffled beat of sound, all the high-pitched guts taken out of the engine note by the wind which swings about us.

Glorious slews into the wind. We can always tell when we're going to fly off, as the big flat-top Bessie goes round in her own length, and the lacy patterns of brine spurting from the bow-wave curve over us as she thrusts her fat tonnage at twenty-five knots across the ridged sea.

Up there a lone pilot is settling his head back against the leather buffer, watching his instruments as he jags the throttle, tightening his head-set strap with the other hand. We can see the director in his bright jersey, yellow against the green-red of the early morning, waving his arms above his head as the Gladiator roars against its chocks, then suddenly he cuts his arms akimbo, down and across, and the Gladiator shoots forward, a grey streak, flinging itself off the bow.

Our eyes follow it as it dips momentarily towards the wave tops, then claws skywards; the pilot taking her round the stern and up past the bridge, up out of our sight.

Ginger McColl shades his eyes as he stares ahead, and he stands there in the wind — a giant of a man, bronze tufts of hair on both cheek-bones. In his blunt Gateshead fashion he says: "Bloody pity the old man didn't send 'em up in the first place. I'd have got me shave in before breakfast..."

Twenty minutes later we get it over the ship's speaker. "Two Ju.'s attacked, one shot down by fighter action, another probable…"

But we don't hear the almighty clatter of the arrester wires until we get back to the mess, stripped to the waist, and fight for places at the hot freshwater tap on the bathroom bulkhead, elbowing for shaving room amid the soap and sweat of thirty others. Then we know the Gladiator is back, but the excitement is over and we are past caring. There is a feeling of disappointment running through the lot of us, and when one of the Fleet Air Arm's flunks says something cocky about the pilots he gets a poke in the privates, which is as much as he deserves for not keeping the tongue quiet in his head.

Well, it would have been darned good to get that Junkers with the guns. Any of the guns.

But especially P.7.

My gun.

Secretly I wonder if Lieutenant Noble, one of the two officers for whom I flunk, would have any bits of gossip to give about the dawn alarm. Not of course that he would think of talking about anything operationally important; but when I go to his cabin I find he hasn't returned. Noble is in charge of the *Glorious'* arrester-gear, among other things; and when a bit later I see him in the wardroom rubbing the stubble on his chin reflectively, I guess the gear has maybe been giving a bit of trouble, so I say nothing. I've got enough trouble on my hands myself anyway. Same as most mornings, when you're on early duty.

I go down the dim passageways, poke my head into the Anteroom — the place we call the Pink Gin Palace — then begin to lay up the tables in the Piggery opposite.

There are two lines of highly polished tables down the fifty-foot length of the wardroom. I know they will be highly polished, because I highly polished them. And I know that slimy little toad of a Maltese messman would bellyache if I didn't keep them that way, though they are covered with white linen at breakfast and lunch, and doilies for dinner, all very Ritzy. Even as a kid when I was in the hotel game, at Gleneagles and the Queen's, Birmingham, I never saw anything Ritzier.

And that is just how this greasy Malt made sure he was kept in the wardroom, because he must have had a fiddle with the officers' catering, like most of the mess-men do, and he wasn't letting a Marine flunk get him caught out. Jobs like that aren't easy to get. Not for men like Josie the Malt.

I lay up the tables and begin to serve breakfast. Even at the best of times the officers come in haphazardly, depending on their duties; but because of this morning's Action Stations things are in a pretty mess. Maunsell, the Surgeon Lieut.-Commander, is among the first in; then the Commander; then my other officer, Lieut.-Commander Hill — that is, the man for whom I flunk in addition to Noble.

Now, no flunkey is long in the Navy or the Royals before discovering that when your officer appears at the breakfast table, the one thing you don't do is go and serve him. You know he'll be away from his cabin for the next twenty minutes at least, so you slide off and make his bunk up. There are the fitted wash-basins to swill round, the slop tank to empty...

A cabin door opposite slams, and I know Ginger Dully is now down here, too, making up the bunk for his man. There's a can of hot water left just outside the door, and I'm going to have a drop of that if I can pinch it off Ginger to save me the long trek along the passageway. I'd like a pound for every scrap we've had together because he's taken the wrong flunk jacket off the hook or because I've lifted his water-can. I'd like a pound for every nosebleed, and for every handshake that brought Ginger back with a grin after the scrapping was over.

A carrier is a rum sort of a place, with its windswept flight-deck, its great grey cliff of steel up to the bridge and its bays of guns. It's a funny place, with its quarterdeck and its wardroom and Pink Gin Palace... its barracks for the Royals, its mess-decks for the matelots, its miles of low-roofed passageways and a thousand coamings to stumble over, its brine-sprayed great hull and all the time its sickly sweet oil stench.

I struggle up the ladders with the slop tank, curse my fat middle as I force the hatch open where I can barely get my elbows through; then walk with the tank outstretched in case I spill it. Too often had a deck-cloth wrapped round my neck for that. In war, we're not supposed to ditch any gash over the side, in case it shows and gives a ship's position away. What the hell do they think we're going to do with the slops. Drink it?

And as I go back through the grey hatch, back through the passageways and near the soft lights of the wardroom, I suddenly realise I've had no proper breakfast, and if I don't look sharp there will be no time now before Cleaning Quarters on the gun at 0900.

They are still having breakfast in the wardroom. I slip in quietly, pick up a silver dish of sausages and walk the length of the room with them, hoping to lift one. But it's in hot fat, hotter than I'd reckoned; and when I let out a soft oath a couple of the officers look up surprised and the Malt hears.

There he is, standing beckoning me out like some imperious head waiter, and because the Malt ranks as a C.P.O., all I can do is mutter: "Sorry, chiefie," because I know he's always flattered when we forget he's only a greasy Malt and call him Chiefie.

"Zat was a sausage you were eating, huh?"

"I didn't eat it, chiefie," I say without conviction. "It was just one in the dish. I'm sorry."

"Zen it stay in zee dish, huh, and you get back and finish off your cabins wiz zee other flunkies. And I'll see Sergeant Healey about it…"

"And I said I'm sorry, chiefie," I repeat. Christ, he's not going to make a song and dance about one damn sausage. And I scarper out while the going's good.

In the passageway Ginger McColl, the one who flunks for the First-Lieutenant, comes up and says: "Don't say I got it from Jimmie the One, but you were right, Tubby. It's going to be Greenock again. With any luck we'll get eight hours."

"Time to give your old woman a bit of cuddle," I say.

"If there's anyone who gets my goat more than Hitler and the captain of this bloody boat," says McColl, eyeing me mournfully, "it's my old woman, and that's straight."

Now, I've been his shipmate for well over two years, and he's always carrying on like that about his old woman.

"I reckon you really worship the ground she walks on," I say, as I always did.

"I'll give her six feet of it, and be right glad to dig it for her, and that's straight."

"Funny you should say that. I was thinking the same about Josie the Malt. I've just about had a gutful of bossing around from that Malt."

"Oh, that newt," says McColl, and makes as if he's going to spit, then remembers where he is. "Wait till you get to Greenock, Tubby. Wait till you get eight ashore. You won't be thinking about him…"

But I am. I'm trying to think of some comeback so sarcastic to give the Malt that it will wipe up the floor with him. But I can't think of it. Not right now.

2

IT wasn't eight in Greenock. It was only four. But, God, was that good…

You didn't have to be even a Galway Bay pilot to feel proud the way *Glorious* was brought in to Greenock after that first Norway run, past Islay and Jura, and Kintyre and Arran, past the lights of Ardrossan and the mouth of Rothesay. And what I remembered more than these lovely sombre colours through the lowering clouds at the water's edge was the grand scent of the fresh sea wind, gathering perfume from the distant rocky highlands and sweeping it down to us over the grassy islands. After the harsh stench of Alex and the Red Sea, this soft grassy air was good to smell.

And now we were in Greenock, and the air was thick with the noises of machinery and the clattering of chains as the *Glorious* took on provisions and fuel, and Hurricane aircraft — their wings like great grey moths broken in the back — were being slung up to the flight-deck, then hustled down to the hangar.

There were a whole lot of us who didn't get shore leave the last time, so we were pretty sure now. Only it was going to be four, not eight. They were loading on these Hurricanes damn fast, which made me more sure than ever that what I'd heard was true — that we were going back straight on the Norway run again. To Narvik, some said.

But right now nothing mattered but those four. And it wasn't going to be more than four for me. Enough of the boys were adrift the last time, and they had to run a special train to Scapa, and take them aboard again when we called there to fly off a squadron.

We hurried along the cobbled dockyard road, the lads dropping off in ones and twos, caught by a fancy shop window — the first English shops we'd seen for over two years — or by the magic of a gust of jukebox music as the door of a tea-joint opened. We hadn't been hearing much music these past months, not even the ship's Marine band.

"What you reckon to do, Tubby?" said the Mangaroo as we strode along the cobbles.

"Mind your business, kid," I said. "Going to enjoy myself."

"Going to do a Micky Bolan?"

Bolan was one of those adrift the last time at Greenock.

"You Irishers," I said. "I'm not that sort of a mug. No, I'm just going to walk around a bit; then maybe get a couple of pints inside me. Mostly I just want to hear people talking a lingo I know, and to go into a shop and order what I want. To give my orders for a change and not be ordered about. It's all right for those couple of hundred lads — the Wavy Navy lot, and the matelots we took on last September in Alex, they haven't had to rough it yet — but I'm darned sick of herrings in tomato sauce and rice like we had all across the Indian Ocean."

"And then for a change rice and herrings in tomato sauce," agreed the Mangaroo. "Makes you thirsty, doesn't it? What do they drink around these parts?"

"A kid like you should stick to the old and mild," I said. "Keep away from the stuff all shining in bottles. Besides, there isn't time for it."

"It's a good whisky I'm after," said the kid; and then with an effort to sound natural: "… and a woman."

"I told you," I said, "there isn't time for it." And I walked on up the dockyard road alone. There was enough going on in my mind, without having to act wet-nurse to the kid.

The woman behind the bar of the tea-joint rested her soft bosom on the counter, dished me out fish and chips and tea, and spoke in a soft burr.

The room was crowded, and all the comfort in the world seemed to be wrapped up in it. There were plenty other than those off the *Glorious*, as I could see from the uniforms, and there were one or two girls, too; but they kept to themselves, and, anyway, I didn't feel like talking to anybody right then. I just wanted to listen.

There was a cup of tea in front of me and not a mug of kye, and there was no need to worry about anything, not even the Malt. Everybody was talking, and I could hardly hear the music for the talk.

I must have been there about half an hour, I reckon, when suddenly through the haze I noticed the clock, and it reminded me I'd better get moving, though I didn't know where to, and I doubt if I'd have got up and left then, only a crowd of others were pushing their way out, and I followed them. Funny, after doing what you're told for so long, you just don't *want* to do what you want to do...

It was cold outside. Not really, I suppose, though it was early April. But it felt cold after the cosy warmth of that tea-joint. And although I hadn't spoken to a soul I remembered in the crowd the face of one girl, her face like as if it was lit by a hidden light, all pretty teeth and smiling. Now I was outside and it felt cold. I walked on, up the street, and others were walking, too, aimlessly like me.

I don't know how long after this it was I found the little pub, and I reckon if I went back to Greenock again today I wouldn't know it, because I didn't so much see it as sense it in the twilight, and because there was warmth and song radiating from the frosted bar window overlooking the cobbles.

The door was thrust open as I came by, showing a yellow-lit glimpse of a wide mahogany bar full of glasses, and a crowd of people in there drinking away as if there wasn't a war on. Then the blackout curtain swung to and the scene was gone. I pushed through the doorway and past the curtain, and there it was, like a painting come to life, all in true colours; but the colours obscured a bit because of the haze of smoke. A piano was going in the snug, and those were the voices I'd heard outside though I didn't know what they were singing:

"*Rose, thee pretty rose so red,*
Rose among the heather..."
Said the youth, "I'll cull thee now,

"Hallo," I said to the red-cheeked girl behind the bar, my eyes on her buxomness.

"And how are you?" she says. "An' what'll ye have?"

"Me? I'm fine, but I'd be better for a pint," I said; and as she pulled it I was thinking of what that Mangaroo kid said; and half of me was looking at her buxomness again and getting her measure, while the other half was angry about the damned injustice of war. Here's this buxom girl in Greenock, and my Peg's a day and a night's journey across the other side of England.

This same side of me was mad that it was only four ashore, and after spring in the Mediterranean I had been longing to gaze on a girl again. But here it wasn't my girl. Not my Peg.

She pushed the glass across the counter with a grin:

"Here's to the next trip, Royal!"

"Here's to you, love," I said, shifting my gaze from her bosom to her eyes. Great wide eyes they were, too. Then down at my beer, where the beads of froth were circling on the brown stream as I gulped thirstily.

In the midst of this crowd at the bar, all pushing for drinks and laughing noisily when they got them, I was lonelier than ever.

I was right glad when I felt a thump on the back, and it was Taff Evanson and another Welshman he'd picked up in the crowd; one of the destroyer matelots it was, whom he knew from last time at Scapa.

"Plain beer," laughed this matelot, "that's no drink for a leatherneck Marine." And pretty soon we were on Jamesons, which isn't ordinarily my drink at all. Not the way this matelot was taking them. Then he and Taff began some argument, goodness knows what it was about now, because I wasn't really listening until suddenly squeaks of laughter went up from some old women on a bench at the back of the crowd, and one said: "Language! Now we're going to hear it," and Taff was shoving the matelot and saying: "Pipe down, sailor. Keep it quiet like…"

That was when I left them and took my glass into the snug. Taff didn't see me go, but the matelot did and he turned round and spoke over his shoulder as if he was spitting.

But I didn't hear the words because of all the talk and the piano was going. Not that it mattered. This matelot was in a state when he couldn't remember whether he'd picked the quarrel with Taff or with me. Not that it mattered…

It was that song which drowned his words. It was a song that sort of came out of the past, and I couldn't remember where I'd heard it before, if ever. Yet I'd seemed always to know it.

> "Rose, thee pretty rose so red,
> Rose among the heather…"
> Said the rose, "My thorn, I vow,
> Thee shall feel. 'Tis sharp now.
> Me thou shalt not gather…"

Edging my way on to the bench at the end of the snug, I began to beat time with my glass, and stared at the crowd around the piano trying to pick the words from their lips. But the words are silly, and at first I don't get the sense of it.

They'd got their arms around each other's shoulders, that crowd by the piano, and then I saw that the buxom girl from behind the bar had come out and was collecting up the glasses, and one of the lads by the piano turned and grabbed at her.

Perhaps she was expecting it or perhaps that dip of her thighs was instinctive, but at any rate she slipped out of his hands and looked back with a high-pitched laugh. And all the time I was thinking of my last Christmas party at home, and the girl who slapped my cheeks when I smacked her buttocks just like it had happened now. Only my girl didn't laugh, and when I pressed her to me she kissed me harder still, like you do at a Christmas party. But that was three Christmases ago.

At first I couldn't place the girl who was standing there with one arm on a feller's shoulder, beating time with her other hand — the girl who kept looking at me with a sideways glance. At first I thought it was the slip of a girl I'd seen in the tea-joint, the girl with the face all lit up and the smiling eyes. But it couldn't be. Anyway, did it matter?

I went over and joined them, and soon she was saying she'd have a drink; and when I'd pushed my way to the bar I made it two Jamesons because it didn't seem right to be drinking beer with a girl. Not a girl like this. Then I made it four Jamesons, to save pushing all through this crowd again. "Make it four, dear," I called.

"Och, now we've got company, have we?" said the buxom one behind the bar, but I pretended not to hear and just spun the money over.

"Here you are, Jock," I said when I got back near the piano, and she gave me a look.

"I'm no Jock, sailor. I'm from Liverpool," she said. "And I'd sooner have had a port. But since you've got it—"

"Sorry, sister," I said, "I'll get you what you want." But as I turned she laid her hand on my arm, quite hard and nice, and told me not to bother. And I said: "Well, now we've got that straight, you're no Jock and I'm no sailor. I'm a time-serving Marine, love, and make no mistake. And in case you're interested, I'm a scouser, too."

"Well I never," she said. "Isn't it a small world — if it weren't that half the folk in Greenock right now come from Liverpool. It's that sort of war, eh, lad?"

"It is an' all," I said. "Well, as one scouser to another: which part?"

She told me, but I didn't catch it because they were singing at the tops of their voices and calling for the encore, so I beckoned to her to come and sit down the other end of the snug. And we sat together and I watched her laugh and sing, and I didn't really know whether I was sorry or glad, but somehow I felt out of it all.

"It's a rum sort of song," I said, when they'd shouted the first verse all over again; but she only laughed again and said: "Come on, boy," and broke into the song:

"… me thee shalt not gather."

"What's it all about?" I said dully. "I can't be sure if I've heard it before. I don't know the words." And she took my hand and began to beat time with it, and I found myself singing.

Under the cover of the song she whispered the words as they fell just a bar ahead, so I could keep in tune. But I wasn't really listening to the singing. I was listening to her soft voice whispering:

"But the youth impatient cull'd
Rose among the heather.
Rose stung sharply as he pull'd,
But her days, alas, were told,
Wounded both together…
Rose among the heather."

"If you're a scouser, how d'you know these Jock songs?" I said at the end; but she was quite sharp and said: "It's not a Jock song, it's just a pretty song about a boy picking a rose. We used to sing it at school."

Then I remembered. But in the council school where we used to sing, it sounded different from the way she sang it.

"… me thee shalt not gather."

"And don't call me a scouser," she said sharply. "That's not a nice word."

"It's what they call us."

"Maybe, but it don't sound too nice. It's an ugly word, an' I don't like ugly things."

"They were ugly times," I said. "Pretty ugly, back in the 'twenties when things were bad and there was only lentil scouse in the pot at home. That's what my dad used to say."

"Forget it," she said, and for a time we just sat there drinking.

Over by the bar a real row was going on, and a couple of the flat-foots were shoved outside, as matelots often are when they've had a skinful. Their shouting echoed up and down in the deserted street outside until I got talking to this girl again, and didn't hear it any more. And it was just as if Peg and I were sitting on that bench in the snug, under the lights and the smoke haze, holding hands — sort of — and talking with our cheeks close so we could hear each other above the singing. Only it wasn't my Peg.

"You married?" she said, and I shook my head.

"Where's your girl, then? She in Liverpool, too?"

"How d'you know I've got a girl?"

"Of course a chap like you's got a girl. Where is she? Has she got a ring?"

"Yes, she's got a ring." I was thinking what a pretty smile she'd got, and wondering if she was having me on, and suddenly she said: "She's lucky."

"You got a regular?" I asked.

"Reg'lar?" She laughed. "What's reg'lar now there's a war on? I haven't seen him since last winter. November it was. I get my ring when he comes back, maybe."

"I haven't seen my girl for more than a couple of years," I said.

And she was quiet for a bit until she asked: "Where d'you meet her, sailor? New Brighton? On the way to Rock Ferry?"

"I tell you," I said. "She isn't from our parts. What d'you care where the hell she comes from anyway?"

"All the same, tell me," she said, and I told her.

I told her how I was with another Marine down by the old Clarence Pier in Portsmouth, and we were broke — well, almost — about threepence left. And Jim Agnew saw a couple of girls over by the Hall of Mirrors in the fun-fair, and began shoving me across, and I felt fed up at being broke and just said: "Oh, to hell with girls," and gave the old punchball another knock.

All the same we went over, and it was Peg and another girl, Pat, and we got talking like kids do, and after that I began writing sloppy letters to her — from places all along the Med, wherever the ship called in.

And I told her how Peg wasn't my first girl, but that I'd always been soft on a kid called Mabel who had grown up together in the same street as me; and that when I took Peg home to meet my mother the other photo had to be shoved quickly away in the sideboard drawer. Then when I got six weeks' leave after docking at Southampton, after coming back from the Med at the time of the Abyssinian trouble, she took me back to meet her mother. As we were waiting for the bus, she blushed and said awkwardly: "By the way, just in case Mum notices. My name's not Peggy. It's Norah."

But I didn't get used to it, and kept calling her Peggy, just the same...

"What about the other one," said the girl at my side. "The one who called herself Pat. That wasn't her real name either, I suppose?"

"No. It was Violet."

"I thought so," she said. "Girls are funny that way…"

"Why? Why?" I said. "What difference does it make? You've got to know some time. Why d'they tell silly lies like that?"

"It's not lies," she said. "You don't know much about women."

We had a few drinks after that, but I kept looking at the clock and knew I'd have to go.

"I'll walk a bit of the way back with you," she said. When we got outside, it was raining and it was pitch black. We stood there, and I put my arm round her to shield off the rain which streamed off my face.

"You don't want to come in this," I said.

"I'll come a bit of the way."

We sheltered half-way, under the granite arches. I wouldn't have done but for the rain. I lit two cigarettes and passed one to her.

"You get sort of lonely," she said.

"I know."

She shivered a bit.

"Cold?"

"No, it was just the rain."

I felt her wrists, then her arms. She felt warm to me.

Something made her draw herself away, but on an impulse I caught her wrists again and drew her against me. Then I bent my head and kissed her, burying my face

35

in her rain-swept hair and the sweet-smelling curve of her neck.

That song was still running through my brain.

"Don't," she said. "I didn't want you to do that." And she pulled herself away from me and ran out into the rain. I could hear her fast-running steps over the cobbles, and for a moment I stood there perplexed; but in the darkness I could see almost nothing, much as I wanted to run after her and say I was sorry and blame it on all those Jamesons.

But it was dark, and I was late. And what the hell anyway.

A torch flashed near my feet, and somebody said: "Hiya, Johnny boy. Johnny. It's me. Beckett."

"Who?" I said dully.

"Johnson — I say, it's me. Beckett." The torch beamed upwards and dazzled my eyes for a moment.

"Sorry, chum. I thought it was somebody I knew. A bloke called Johnnie. Sorry to spoil your fun."

I stared into the torchlight, and guessed he must have heard her running footsteps.

"Oh her," I said. "That wasn't…"

Then I shut up, because there was really nothing to say that wouldn't sound just blamed silly, not with me standing there in the darkness and the rain and the girl running away.

"You Marines!" he said with a short laugh. "Lucky perisher."

We walked on a few yards together until we reached the gates and I could see who he was.

A rating pilot, lumping a load of his kit. I reckoned it was one of the new pilots we were taking on to fly the Hurriboxes out to Norway. Well, thank Christ for that. The *Glorious* is a big place, and he'd be in a different world from me and probably I'd never see him again once we were aboard. Thank Christ for that. Well, I didn't want anybody to take the mickey.

3

A GOOD flunk keeps his trap shut. Well, it's a dead cert when you flunk for the officers you're bound to hear a thing or two.

In the wardroom they don't gab about anything much except their troubles at home, which are just like ours only worse. But when men begin to talk even about the general conduct of the war, by putting two and two together you can learn a lot about what goes on behind the scenes. Anyway, you knew more about the war than they printed in the *Daily Mirror*. To read it you'd have thought the *Ark Royal* was the only aircraft-carrier in the whole blamed Navy.

When you got letters from home, so cockeyed wrong about the war, it hurt, and you longed to be able to write back to Mum, or to Peg, and tell where the fighting was really happening and what the *Glorious* was up to. At Greenock twice we missed the mail-boat, but usually our letters weren't more than a fortnight late, and that applied to the papers, too. In war-time it doesn't make much difference if the headlines are two weeks' old or fresh as yesterday. It's the same old bunk. It used to get the skipper's goat.

There was a chap writing that Hitler had too many submarines and that aircraft-carriers were out of date and too easy to hit, and I happened to be in the wardroom when this started a proper argy-bargey because if there's one thing a man like the skipper can't stand is being told his job by a shore-based pen-shover. Captains like D'Oyly Hughes don't get their D.S.O. ribbons to wear just as a bit of fancy decoration.

"Wanted — Enormous Offensive Fleet," one of the chaps was reading, then slapped the paper as viciously as if the writer of that headline was wrapped up in it.

"Offensive fleet, my backside. It's the bastard himself who's being offensive."

"You want to read between the lines," said one of the other subs. "No use taking that tripe for what it says. It's all playing politics. You know — one of the Press Lords trying to tell the Admiralty how to run the war when they don't know how to run their own tomfool newspapers."

"Yes, but all this cock about submarines. I thought it was common knowledge that Hitler had only about seventy U-boats when the war started, and that with our C and D Class light cruisers we've enough to enforce the blockade."

"Looks like they've got the wind-up about surface raiders," someone suggested. "You know — when the *Graf Spee* sank the *Clement* off Pernambuco. They say there was one hell of a fuss when the survivors landed in Brazil. Didn't even seem to know what hit 'em."

"Depends what this chap means by an offensive fleet. After all, we've got our chaps strung out from the Atlantic convoys to Sumatra and Sierra Leone. Don't mind admitting, if any Press Lord or any ruddy politician starts a campaign to get more carriers, I'm all for it. Carriers are bloody ugly, with their unbeautiful bows hidden by the flight and their rounded-down stern like a duck's backside; but when you're driving into a thirty-knot wind, my lad, there's real rakish beauty for you, and you can keep all your destroyers and ocean greyhounds."

"Beauty, Hugh? You're always trying to see beauty in everything."

"There's plenty of beauty in war, especially the war at sea, if you keep your weather-eye skinned. Ever seen a picture lovelier than when even a flat-topped old barmaid like this is shuddering with speed, shaking the water from her scuppers in cascades of foam? There's as much grace and beauty when the bang-boxes trigger off and the whole scene's covered in purple smoke as any sunset by an Old Master."

"Time for that when this lot's over," someone cut in. "Then you can get back to your Chelsea garret and sketch it all from many happy memories, as a change from painting popsies in the raw. But this lot's not over yet. Far from it.

"It isn't just politics or preaching. The Navy's simply got to use all its air weapons to strike at strategic targets, and that's where carriers come in. Mobility's our strong-point, you know, and because we can be moved in the shortest time to whatever point of attack is vital, we can deliver an equal weight of bombs more economically than shore-based aircraft."

"We're a long way off having enough aircraft able to drop more than a tin-can on Jerry."

"It'll come. This lot's not over by a long way yet."

"Meantime we're vulnerable."

"I don't see how you can say that a carrier which can move at least five hundred miles in twenty-four hours is any easier a target than a shore-based airfield which you can pick out as a sitting target."

And so they'd argue on.

Now, one reason why Ginger Woollon and I knew a bit more about the conduct of the war than the coots who write in the papers is that we had the best Jewin' job in *Glorious*. We were ship's barbers.

Ginger was a three-badge Marine, a real old sweat, and he had cut hair before. He put me up to it. The first time I'd ever cut any man's hair was when we were at Plymouth barracks, and somebody got picked up for a hair-cut when the shops were shut, so we just went to it with nail-scissors. And I learned to cut hair. It was one of the best fiddles of the lot, even considering that in a ship like the *Glorious* there are plenty of Jewin' jobs, such as photography and dhobi-wallah.

They weren't for me. I don't understand anything about cameras, and doing the washing's not much of a lark if you can get anybody to do it for you. So we stuck to cutting hair.

Two bob for the officers, a tanner for the others. Those were our prices. We had a little space at the end of the mess-deck between the sergeants' horsebox — that's their mess — and the Marine band's mess. Funny thing how many little bits of waste ground there are in a ship the size of the *Glorious*. We found ours all right.

We scrounged two stools, and then we rigged up a string of four electric bulbs. When he wasn't flunking for the Senior Engineer — which to his way of thinking was always too often — Ginger helped me cut hair. A chubby, red-faced and friendly type. I never did get to know just where in the West Country he hailed from. Maybe it's Plymouth. But with that soft and friendly West Country burr, you got talking to him and you opened your heart. People do, anyway, in the barber's chair. That's how we got to know so much about what was going on.

I wouldn't like to say just when and where I heard it all, but we'd two very good reasons for wanting to know. For one thing, we were sick to the ears of all the rot about the *Ark Royal*, and that's why they called her the *Daily Mirror* ship. The other was that we'd been two and a half years in commission, chasing Raeder or Raeder's ghost through the Indian Ocean and the Red Sea, and after this third Norway run it was going to be bottoms up and a damned good picnic for all. Maybe for six weeks.

Now, you didn't need to read the papers to know things were not going well in Norway, or in France either for that matter.

All the time we'd been out in the Aden area, along with the *Malaya* and *Ramillies* and Australian destroyers, *Furious* and *Repulse* had been doing the Atlantic convoy job. *Ark Royal* and *Renown* were off Freetown; *Cornwall*, *Dorsetshire* and *Eagle* were covering Colombo and Ceylon. That was stretching things tight and wide.

Ajax and *Achilles* were east of South America. *Berwick* and *York* were covering North America and the West Indies, and in addition to the *Kent* and *Suffren* off Sumatra, we had *Revenge*, *Resolution*, *Warspite*, *Emerald* and *Effingham*

— and maybe others — on North Atlantic convoy patrol. That's how the picture was when suddenly after weeks of herrings in tomato sauce and rice, we got the signal bringing us back from Aden and hastily re-equipping at Scapa. And for what?

"And for what, I'd like to know?" Ginger used to ask himself, squatting on the stool when there weren't any more customers and making a prique of tobacco as he spoke. "Now we're under the orders of the C.-in-C. Home Fleet, just like the *Ark Royal*. And it means Norway again. And for what, Tubby?"

"'Support of military operations' it says on Orders," I volunteered. "Nobody's paid to tell us what it's all about. Just put your drip-tin on, and don't moan about it."

"Yes, Tubby. But I've got a theory," said Ginger. "Now, look, it's like this prique here." And so saying he spread the little canvas cloth and the roll of baccy on the bench.

"This bit of canvas's Norway. See? And this Tickler's is Hitler — not that that perisher is half so good-looking as an empty Tickler's baccy-tin. Now, look. I take my baccy out of the tin and I pull the stems off the leaves. That gives us the best of it, just like Hitler has saved the best of his lot for Norway. Then what do I do? I sprinkle it with me rum ration, just like Hitler soaks his hand-picked Panzers with the best equipment he's got, and there they are in Norway."

He folded the canvas cloth on the rum-soaked Tickler's and pulled it tight.

"Norway, Tubby. All mountains and fjords and rough edges. Not a nice place to be squeezed up in. Not a nice place at all." And he gave the cloth another twist so the rum smelled sweet. And another twist. And another.

"Now, what am I going to do with this prique, Tubby? Why, I'm going to keep it maybe two months. Maybe three. With the Tickler's squeezed up in there just like we're going to keep Jerry squeezed up in Norway. And then? Then the lot's going up in smoke, the same as this prique'll go up in smoke in my pipe. You see…?"

This theory didn't seem so good in the small hours when you were doing sub. look-out. When it's Cruising Stations, only a quarter of the ship is on duty. When it's Defence Stations, half is up. Four hours on, four off. You get pretty tired, and the war doesn't seem at all so neatly tied up in a bundle as Ginger's prique of tobacco.

Sub. look-out is a bit of a racket, because there should be two awake on duty from each gun-crew. Maybe it'd be Jerry Rotherby, or Taff, or Mickey, or one of the others, and you don't need four eyes to look for one perishing periscope. Then one of us would go off to the galley and come back with a fannyful of kye, that murky ship's cocoa so swirling in fat the spoon stands up straight in the fanny.

Hour after hour you'd be looking out over the guard-rail, scanning the wheel of the horizon with eyes that burned, peering into the empty face of the ocean. Suddenly you thought it was a periscope, and kicked the chap by you who should be awake. But always it's only phosphorus, and the flecks of foam ride on and away as the *Glorious* edges towards Norway.

We weren't the only ones dead-beat. On the first Norway run the clatter of arrester wires was going all the time as the Swordfish came back after nonstop two-hour patrols. And our chaps had been flying all the time at Narvik. We were sweating at our own jobs as we watched the fighters cant over in the bank, then almost finger the sea before climbing off for the Norwegian coast. The boys used to say it was nerve-racking getting out of the way of our own ack-ack as well as Jerry's shore batteries.

It wasn't until the third Norway run that we struck a twenty-four action, and I prayed we'd never get another.

There'd been a lot of air activity all the previous night, and I had been on sub. look-out, trying to keep my eyes on the phosphorous ridges of grey green, but often as not looking skywards as the Hurriboxes came in one by one to land.

They came in close astern, seeming as they canted over in the bank almost to be at a standstill for one split second, though actually doing better than a hundred knots. Then you'd see the pilots clambering down from the flight-deck and into *Glorious'* cavernous depths: into the debriefing room, to tell the story of what they'd seen over the Norwegian coast. It was pretty sure things were hotting up. You could tell that, too, by the mechanical hammerings coming all night from the hangars, where some of the Swordfish were struck down for maintenance as the other fighters were operational. The racket seemed to fill the whole ship, and I didn't sleep too well that night.

I must have been wide awake for half an hour or so, cursing that dull thudding, cursing the way we felt so cold now at nights after the Aden trip and our blood being thinned down, cursing Josie the Malt who threatened he'd have me on the hooks for an officer-chit which ought to have been signed but wasn't.

Then, in the middle of it all, came Action Stations.

Don't know why, but the thought flashed through my mind: "Wonder which of those kids is sounding it?"

There were two Marine buglers, both kids. One about fifteen, the other maybe a year older. One was a little ginger kid, the other dark and curly. As soon as it was Action Stations, one of those kids was on the bridge, and the Tannoy was switched on to the speakers relaying it to every part of the ship. Even the closets.

It was just the same at all the main calls — at mail call, at the rum issue at 1100 and all the rest of it. Or you'd hear the bo'sun's whistle wailing up and down and the order would come over: "Hands to muster on quarterdeck..." or "First part of port watch..."

You got so used to the old rigmarole that you acted instinctively. But Action Stations is different. It isn't fear that halts you for a moment. I don't know what it is. But you stop and think, and maybe you say a little prayer.

We got out to P.7, dragging on our seaboots and struggling into lifebelts, grabbing Tickler's, bits of chocolate or anything else you could jam into your pockets. No knowing how long you'd be out there. Why did the bastards always begin it before breakfast...?

The sky was green and threatening, the sort of green that mirrors the choppy sea at this early hour, and as we stepped up to the gun platform and caught the force of the dawn wind it cut right through your bones, penetrating the jerseys and woollen llamis. Maybe we just felt it keener, after Aden; I wouldn't know.

Ready-use ammo. Locker open. Check the star-shells, check the armour-piercing. Get round the gun. Switch on. Get your first batch of projjies out and fuse to zero. Then wait. And go on waiting. Waiting for the order that doesn't come.

In another hour or maybe two the pale sun would come over the horizon and set the waves glistening, driving away the fringe of mist that tinged the green dawn sky with silver. And, like we were waiting for the sun, the whole ship was expectant, alone in what might either be majesty or danger... alone except for the stray wisps of smoke, tell-tales of our escorting destroyers *Acasta* and *Ardent*. And they said the anti-sub.-trawler *Juniper* was somewhere out there, too, but giving no tell-tale. *Glorious* ploughed on, rigging whining, giant bow plating trembling, screws pulsing.

"If the bastards must get us up in the dark," said Jerry, "I wish we'd have a bit of luck and get a raider. Something juicy, like the *Graf Spee*. I'd give all I've got to see the fireworks when we put a group of star-shells up over her and silhouette her against the dark before we blew the guts out of her. Yes, it'd be a pretty sight, having her lit up by star-shells."

"I've never even seen a practice round of star-shells fired, and that's the truth," said the Mangaroo sadly.

"Well, I can't say as I've ever seen one fired in anger, as you might say," said Jerry. And, as it happened, we never did.

"Might be the old *Graf Spee* round the corner this morning. Or something hefty like the Salmon and Gluckstein," said Jock.

"Break it up. Ever heard you shouldn't defy the Fates?"

"O.K., O.K. But it'd be good to meet up with something worthwhile, like that pair of bastards. They've got eleven-inchers on the *Scharnhorst* and *Gneisenau*, I believe. Eight or nine of them. And a batch of five-point-nines. Now that's stuff worth taking on, I ask you."

"Break it up, like I said."

Then the orders began to come through, and the Marine Band boys who operated T.S. stations in action got busy. The misty green sea was stirred up to thunder, and I stared over the guard-rail at the vicious snouts of purple-red while the air was thick with so much clatter it sort of hit you in the belly. And there we were standing idle. P.7 could not bear.

"For Christ's sake, give us a chance," yelled Taff. "Give us a few rounds local-fire and we'll show the perishers."

Then he got his wish.

"*Report your target…*" "*Enemy in sight…*" "*Target bear red four-five… range three thousand… open fire…*"

It's always that first burst from P.7 which I find stupefying. The violent crash, the electrifying recoil, then the burst of flame which makes you gasp. Then after a bit you get accustomed to the noise and can hear the shell screeching and whinneying away into space; and the reek of cordite acts on you like alcohol.

Then silence.

Having got our elevation, fused a batch of projjies and fired a few rounds, we felt a bit better, even though we hadn't shot the arse-feathers off a seagull. But it's the inaction you don't like. For one thing, it breaks up the teamwork.

It's teamwork in a gun-crew, on P.7 just as on all the other guns, and if you get just one nervous guy it puts the whole team out. The Mangaroo kid used to suffer that way until we got him out of it.

He used to stand there, head down, just waiting, instead of nipping in and helping to get those projjies moving from the ammo supply hoist to second supply, then to second fuse-setter, then to me. Then to the loader, and up on to the tray. That's the chain of teamwork.

The kid used to stand there, head down, scared to move.

"This is a fine time to split your trousers, man, straight it is," yelled Taff, and we burst out laughing. Even the kid began to laugh. You can't laugh and be afraid, not both at the same time. And that did the trick.

"That Mangaroo. He should have been a girl," said Ginger. But I shut him up. I was scared, and so were most of the others, I reckon; but we showed it differently and tried to kid ourselves it didn't show at all.

This waiting. I didn't like it. Then we got word round a high-level attack was beginning, and eyes were strained to the sky. The sense of crisis gave you a new kick, and we shook our fists up to the green sky and shouted at the invisible target: "Come down, you bastards. You're all right up there…!"

They came down all right. Ju. 88's they were, and they came down in a steep dive. I could see the tracer bullets going at them from our pom-poms… then not more than fifty yards behind our Skuas were on their tails. Two minutes and it was all over. Twenty minutes and it started again.

"*Switch to local-fire.*" All around us in the sea stood green-grey spouts of water, some of the gunners or maybe the T.S. boys having lost their heads and the guns firing too late on the upward roll. We'd have to do better than this.

Then waves of the ruddy things began coming over, and we got the local-fire call from T.S. for half an hour at a stretch.

"*Zero fuse, rapid fire,*" called the layer, and we went to it like a lot of cold, sweating navvies to get plenty of projjies in the air, no matter where. But all the time the trainer was slewing the gun round, looking along his sights.

We had about four hours of this before the lads got a break.

"Doesn't give you time for a tom-tit," moaned Ginger, but it wasn't that which worried me. I was hungry. It was in the fifth hour we managed to get one of the lads to the galley to draw rations. One big meat dish, it was, with spuds and some other mucked-up veg. And half a loaf. And there was always kye on the go. In the hurry at Action Stations only Jock and I thought to bring our eating-irons, so we all pigged in. It wasn't a very big dish.

The attack slacked off around midday, and we kept flying aircraft off and on.

"I don't much like it," commented Jerry. "We flew a squadron off at Scapa, remember? Looks like the old man knew we were going to take on more when we got back on the Norway run. But these aren't Hurriboxes. They're all Skuas and Swordfishes, and some are from the *Daily Mirror* packet, I think, by their markings. If we're taking them back on, I don't like the look of it. What's happening out there, eh?"

We knew by nightfall. We'd sent Gladiators from *Glorious* to Lake Lesjeskogen, the frozen lake making a good emergency air-strip. And now Skuas and Swordfish from the *Ark Royal* and from us were flying 90 miles inland protecting British troops, while others made a mass attack on Trondheim, in fog and snow.

As it got dusk again, the Ju.'s came back. They came back in a sinuous curving dive, and we gave them all the red-hot metal we'd got, a crazy crash of controlled broadsides, with jags of flame until the whole area around the *Glorious* was wreathed in flame-shot smoke.

It was when I went for the tea ration that I felt rather than heard the rattle of cannon-shell, and looking back a few yards I saw the steel plate of the ship ripped open in a straight line. I felt like laughing, because somehow I knew it wasn't for me. Not on my copybook.

I got back to the gun with that fannyful of tea, and I was singing a snatch of a song to myself.

"Rose stung sharply as he pulled,
But her days, alas, were told,
Wounded both together…"

Yet, if I'd been asked, I wouldn't have known what I was singing. By the end of that twenty-four-hour action, we were dead-beat, and we struck bad weather after that and didn't get much sleep for another night and day.

I was kept pretty busy flunking, too, as both my officers, Noble and Hill, were on duty watch or stand-off watch, so often were not in the wardroom with the others, and I had to get the chores done when I could.

Noble, Lieutenant (E.), was small, dark and wiry, and a very good sort though not too familiar; a different cup of tea from Lieutenant Jouchin, the Lieutenant (E.) for whom I'd flunked before the war. We were such buddies I even used to borrow his hockey and football boots — with him knowing. Noble didn't like to talk.

All during the night flying — and through this first grim twenty-four-hour action — he had his meals up in the pilots' shelter, and when I could I used to get them up there in a wooden box affair to keep the stuff hot. Hill — Lieut.-Commander Hill — I didn't know so much about, except that we picked this big-built and generous man up at Colombo, where he joined the *Glorious*. I'd always had the idea he was a tea-planter out there, and joined the carrier again when he knew the Service needed him. Right or wrong, I got the idea he was retired from the Navy then came back. There was plenty to do for Hill and Noble after the action, and I didn't waste time talking.

That bad weather we struck came a bit tough after the action. I was never sick in the *Glorious*, but as a flat-top she certainly could roll. I don't know why, but I'd always been all right ever since I went out in the *Lancashire* to Alex. Maybe it was because I used to take care and try to get a kip if I felt queer.

Taff, always one for a song, loved to pull my leg and hum something from a Gilbert and Sullivan opera:

"But when the breezes blow,
I generally go below,
And seek the seclusion that a cabin grants!
And so do his sisters,
   And his cousins
     And his aunts…"

But they were singing to the wrong one, because it was a real old sweat, a time-serving Marine, who soon became the butt of us all because he spewed his heart up if *Glorious* so much as rolled. We never saw him once we ran into bad weather.

"Where's old so-and-so?" we'd ask, but nobody'd seen him or were likely to. But I always knew where he was. There was a hot-water tank between the mess-deck and the Marines bathroom, and that's where he was, hidden under a pile of old coats, moaning. You'd lift the coats up, and there he was, moaning "Let me die."

Nobody said: "Let me die" when the Ju.'s were dive-bombing; but the sea can do it to you, and then you don't fight against death. You pray for it. It's an old saying: "A seasick arse keeps no watch…"

For me, I didn't care about the bad weather we ran into: I figured it would keep off another twenty-four-hour action. And then in a week or two we'd be the other side of the North Sea, with several weeks' leave on the horizon. Until then, the more bad weather the better.

4

I WON'T easily forget the climax of *Glorious'* part in the defence of Norway, when Trondheim was raided again and again, and our Skuas and Swordfishes drilled their way through Ju. and Heinkel opposition, then came back to their mother carrier to refuel before chasing off again nearly a hundred miles inland.

It was the first time in history that carrier-borne aircraft were used in prolonged operations of this nature, and I could tell from wardroom talk that all the time our Fleet Air Arm boys were hopelessly outclassed by the shore-based aircraft opposed to them. There were cheers in the mess when we learned that the C.-in-C. Home Fleet, in forwarding the report of the Vice-Admiral Aircraft Carriers to Downing Street, scribbled on the signal: "… *And the sooner we get some efficient aircraft the better.*"

We hoped this would be the end of the first commission, and that all in the *Glorious* would get at least six weeks ashore. But no. Bloody murder was going on in Norway. We'd have to do one more run. And then maybe we'd get our shore leave. Maybe…

After a brief respite at Scapa and the Clyde to make good aircraft losses, we were ordered to the Narvik area, and a few days later learned that the *Ark Royal* was on the same run. Now perhaps we'd get *our* pictures in the *Mirror*…

But she was never more than a speck on the horizon to us, as, Action Stations after Action Stations, we were at our gun-positions throughout the final evacuation of Norway in June. The *Ark Royal* was, in fact, providing fighter protection, while *Glorious* was evacuating the Hurricanes.

These were the days when the air war was critical, and I guess there were many heroic deeds then, not mentioned even in Admiralty records. From the pilots returning to the *Glorious* we heard of several. Lesjeskogen, for instance.

Lesjeskogen is a frozen lake midway between Aandalsnes and Dombas, and a week or so back the *Arethusa* had left Rosyth with R.A.F. staff and stores for the lake, arriving secretly at Aandalsnes within twenty-four hours. Then we rendezvoused, three days later, by which time the Brylcreem boys had swept the whole lake clear of snow and brought in their radar and other gear. Later we flew off eighteen R.A.F. Gladiator aircraft, with the idea of using the lake as an air-strip for attack.

Jerry got to hear of it, and by the next morning nearly all the aircraft had been destroyed in Ju. dive-bomb attacks, though our lads shot down ten of them, and kept on shooting even with their Sten guns until at last all but a handful of the R.A.F. was left. The undamaged remainder of the Gladiators limped back to the *Glorious*...

After the worst of the Trondheim attacks, the Admiralty sent us a signal:

"We are proud of the Fleet Air Arm," it read.

"Bugger the Fleet Air Arm," sniffed Ginger who was with me when the signal was relayed. "I suppose they think the rest of us are just out here for the ride."

It was at the end of a twenty-four-hour action when we'd been round the gun a whole night and a day, red-eyed, half choked with cordite, hungry, and scarred from shell-splinters. Nobody wants to be a bloody hero, but you just go on doing your job.

It wasn't Hitler who was getting me down, but the toothache. Cully, flunk to Pierce, the Surgeon-Lieutenant (D.), kept telling me I ought to have the bad one filled, but I put it off and off because for one thing it seemed a bit damn silly reporting sick for toothache in the middle of an action. And, for another, Pierce had to take his watch on the bridge with the others, as well as pulling teeth, so he wasn't around much.

At last it became so acute I simply had to go to him, and although I knew Pierce from wardroom duty as a good-natured young Irishman, I was surprised to discover that his shop was fitted up with all the latest gadgets. The toothie's shop was right under the flight-deck, starboard, a little aft. I settled down under the lamps and that damn drill, and would hardly have known I was not back in my little front-parlour dentist's in Liverpool, except that the *Glorious* was heading at 30 knots, and from that alone I might have known something was cooking.

Pierce had his left hand steadying my jaw, his right holding the drill, when the first crack came — a slam like the whip of a giant steel thong strapping the *Glorious'* flight-deck. Then it came again.

Turning my eyes without daring to move my head, for the toothie did not let his hand falter, I could see through a square port what it was. The arrester wires come through the bulkhead by the toothie's shop, and as each aircraft was hugged to a standstill by the great steel cables there was a crack like a gun, then the horrible drawn-out roar of the hydraulic rebound cylinders. It was like sitting in the middle of the mechanism of an express locomotive, but Pierce's hand did not tremble. He never let the drill dig in... and at last I managed to sit through it. But, as I say, it's the little damn things in war that hurt. Like toothache.

It was around this time, too, that many of us were undergoing the wearying experience of ranging from the crest of happiness to the trough of misery: the misery of a two-and-a-half-year commission made so much longer by the outbreak of war. The crest of happiness when the commission seemed nearly at an end and I could be back with the family again, making plans with Peg for our marriage before the summer was out.

The nearer we reached the end of the show, the more touchy we became, and the mounting frequency of Action Stations tensioned us, made life more grossly uncomfortable than it might have been — then, illogically, left us when each attack was over, not content but fretful and morose. The same feeling was spreading through the ship. We'd all be glad when this lot was over.

Around the time when we didn't get an action for eighteen hours at a stretch, I decided to get a bath. With all the dirt and sweat around the gun, a bath ought to be easy; and when you get Action Stations several times in each twelve hours most of us sleep in our clothes, deado, and don't bother to take off more than our shoes. So I needed that bath.

But the bathroom is at the end of the henhouse, and there isn't room to swing a cat. There are four hand-basins, one lukewarm salt shower, and on the bulkhead one warm fresh-water tap. And six galvanised baths,,... Queueing to get in, queueing to grab hold of a tin bath, fighting to drag your half-filled bath to a space... bending down to wash without getting the next man's backside in your soapy eyes.

To make it worse, that night I was duty flunk, which meant dressing again, doing wardroom duty, then getting back for my meal half an hour or more after everything was cold. It's little things like that they don't tell you about when you sign on for twelve to see the world... I never figured why they think the Marines won't grouse as much as the flat-foots, yet it's a fact: no matter how a ship is arranged, the Marines' mess always separates the officers from the matelots. That's traditional, from the days when the crew might mutiny, but the Marine was a sworn-in man to keep order.

Maybe the Royals in those days didn't get a twenty-four action round a gun. Maybe they had their mail regular, not waiting as I was for three weeks' for a letter from Peg.

Maybe there wasn't so much bull in those days.

The bull. I guess *Glorious* was no worse than the rest. But you'd think we had to polish that bloody boat to make her float. In our mess there were long tables, twenty-four men to each. One end of each table was hinged to the hull-plates, the other was supported on crawfords. Above were the hammock bars, the hammocks not being stowed at all in war. There was supposed to be plenty of time to polish the tables and all the tinware and the fanny you got the tea in — all stored in the wedge-shaped cupboards at the table ends, wedge-shaped to prevent the crocks breaking when the ship rolled. You polished the lot. Even the hanging crawfords. That's the sort of bull it was.

My locker and mess table were near the Marine office, where Tim Healey sat brooding on the equipment and the sick reports, and that's the reason my bit of bull was tougher than the others. Healey was a good scout, and played tombola with the boys at nights. But it was his job to lay on the bull, and I reckon I'd have been the same in his job. Not that I ever would have been. Marines are cast in different moulds, I suppose, and I was never cut out to be a sergeant.

Little things get my goat: like when I got back that night and all the dinners were dished up and the stuff was cold, and my jaw was still sore from that goddam drill of Pierce's, and it was about time they called this whole bloody war off. That night I'd got my drip-tin on good and square.

It was pretty late when I got into my hammock, throwing my second blanket along the cleats, then tucking it in under me like a mummy. And there I lay, thinking it all out... watching Jock Clark with the patience of Job filing his bit of brasswork, which he always did for hour after hour at sea to take his mind off.

Off what? I never knew. When not filing that silly bit of brass he was writing pages and pages of letters home. I never knew what he found to put in them, or what she wrote back that left him so blissful in his private thoughts, just swaying back and forth as he sat there, filing that bit of brass until he clogged the file, then patiently rubbing the file with his brass comb...

Jerry Rotherby and Mickie Bolan were going on and on about some long-lost or long-won battle in the Med. Jerry was the best water-polo player we'd got, and Mickie, although a Marine, was about the best sailor I'd met. Out East he entered all the regattas for sailing-boats, gigs and cutters, devil-may-care, and beat all the officers, who loved him when he was sober and forgave him when he wasn't. I put up with their ragging for a long time, so it seemed, until I had to give them a for-Christ-sake.

Well, I wanted to get a bit of sleep, as we'd be certain to get Action Stations before dawn. But we didn't, funnily enough. Not that time.

It came at tea-time next day.

I'd just finished in the wardroom when we started taking on more Hurricanes after they'd scoured the hell out of the Norway Panzers. The *Glorious* began to get up tremendous speed into the wind, to help the Hurriboxes land. Round they'd come at about 200 feet so we could see they were O.K. to come in, then they'd circuit again and line up for the landing, coming in with a mighty gust and a lather of spray.

One by one the pilots dragged themselves out, loosening their harness and vaulting down to the flight-deck to be received for the official debriefing. I had a slack half-hour after wardroom duty, as both my officers were busy, Hill on the upper deck concerning himself with stowage of gear, and Noble in the pilot's shelter on the flight-deck, helping to wheel and land them in out of the clear sky. The sea was calm and deep blue; a good June day for the Arctic...

It was at that moment they sounded off Action Stations, and from my point by the flight-deck I could see it was the little dark kid sounding the bugle. Then the alarm gongs went like mad, enough to wake the dead out of an afternoon's sleep.

I was in shirt and vest, so I had to fight my way through the running crowd of men down to the henhouse, grab my seaboots, tin helmet and the couple of bars of chocolate which experience by now taught me were worth more than baccy during a long action.

I'd gone back down a couple of ropes when once again I realised I'd forgotten that goddam lifebelt. On a hunch, I went back, and there was the ugly thing, half inflated in locker 86 as I always kept it. Premonition made me grope inside the locker for my photos, and then I laughed to myself as I remembered the Mangaroo kid doing just the same on the first Norway run. It was a confounded nuisance going back for that lifebelt, because I couldn't get my locker door shut. Something seemed to have battered the thin sheet-iron door out of true, and I struggled with it for maybe a couple of minutes until I daren't wait any longer because they needed me down there to start fuse-setting the projjies. But I was annoyed about that darned door. When I came back after the action, I didn't want to find my things all over the mess-deck.

They were waiting for me on P.7.

"Jesus, Tubby, you pick a fine time to go and lock yourself in the bog, and that's the truth."

It was the Mangaroo. I was a bit glad to find he was still cracking a joke, and not scared after the fairly non-stop actions of the past weeks.

And Jerry, a bit closer to me even than some of the others, just asked quietly: "Nothing wrong, was there, Tubby?"

"No," I said. "Only my bloody locker. The door's jammed. I'll have to look at it when we get back."

"And a damn long while that's likely to be, indeed," said Taff Evanson peevishly. "Not a blamed order's come through yet."

Well, we were all querulous. It was a nice afternoon, and you don't often get the Arctic as calm as this, not even in June. And we wanted our tea.

Ready-use ammo. Fuse-tray out, pinned and locked. Fuse the first few projjies. Then stand around, just wondering when the dive-bombing attack's going to begin. You light a dog-end, then stub it out again after a minute because you're too on edge to draw at it. You wanted to light up just to give your fingers something to do.

Only Jock is at peace, swaying away at his bit of brass with that damned pocket file. I begin a crazy tattoo with the fuse-spanner on the unprotesting end of a shell-case, until Ginger hollers to me to stop.

It's about time they came. What's Wells waiting for? Perhaps the T.S. Marine Band boys are waiting for a band-call and have forgotten to relay the orders. What are we waiting for? What the hell are we waiting for?

Somebody came running, somebody from the adjoining gun-bay. He was passing the signal round.

"Holy Pete!" yelled Jerry, who got the meaning of it first. "It's the Salmon and Gluckstein. Well, thank God for that. It'll be a nice change from Goering's bastards…"

"I wonder, man," conjectured Taff quietly. "They do say the *Scharnhorst* has got eleven-inchers."

"That's what I bloody told you," said Jock. "Nine of 'em, and a darned whole lot of five-point-nines. I tell you, if this is the Salmon and Gluckstein, it isn't so funny. Not with us and our four-point-sevens."

"Aw, the beer-garden buggers couldn't hit us even if they had stuff the size of the *Rodney*."

Then there was quiet, with everybody tense.

Now, if it had been the sky-high drone of Ju.'s, I'd have been crazily zero-fusing those projjies for local firing, sweating on the top line that Ginger would get his elevation right first time, and we'd do a bit of four-point-seven pigeon-shooting. But not this time. Just quiet. A quietness you could almost feel.

I reckon we were making nearly thirty knots, and *Glorious* was shuddering with speed. But I didn't know it. I was thinking. Ugly thoughts they were.

Come to think of it, there must have been a lot of a rowdy jumble going on, because there was so much thudding of machinery, and the cutting of the wind, and the shouting of brisk orders, that we hardly heard the first salvo above it. You got so used to this conglomeration of sounds in the *Glorious* you didn't notice they were going on... until the crash of a shell put your familiar rhythm out of tempo, and there was all this noise at once, hitting you with its stark ugliness.

The flight-deck above us was wreathed in smoke, then tongues of flame, then the staccato sounds of fire rose to a great roar, and a red wall like a living furnace rose from the hangar-well.

Our backs to this inferno, we gazed out over the horizon, where the enemy ships — if it had been these that had struck — could not be seen, and the escorting *Acasta* and *Ardent* were circling the edge of sky and sea, obliterating both with a frenzied smoke-screen.

We just stood there, looking at each other — Jerry and Ginger, and the Mangaroo kid and the rest. This wasn't the war we knew. They'd given us our four-point-seven to fight with, but this wasn't fighting. This was murder. Sudden, blazing dirty murder.

"I wouldn't like to be in the old man's place for a fortune," said Jock suddenly.

"I don't think so much of ours, neither."

"No, but I mean if our range is so much less than the eleven-inchers, then all he can do is get the Swordfishes up with torpedoes, and a damn fine chance he'll have of doing that with the hangar blazing like bloody hell."

"Would only take one tin-fish to sink either the Salmon or the Gluckstein. Anyway, if the destroyer boys can get in close…"

"Who says it's the Salmon and Gluckstein anyway? Probably the American Navy's decided to join in the war, and they didn't 'guess-an'-calker-late' with their first shot."

Then it came again, like distant thunder, culminating in a sudden wall of vicious sound, leaving the whole gun platform shuddering with the impact. Merciful God, they'd got their range right …

I looked up the cliff face of the wall of steel forward of the bridge and saw the steel shattering. Plumets of smoke filled the air as I watched in horror. They'd hit the bridge. At the impact, I threw myself on the platform instinctively.

We waited on maybe a couple of minutes.

"This is bloody silly," shouted Ginger above the roar of flames. "There's nothing we can do here. Let's scram up and do what we can about the hangar fire."

"But orders…" said Taff stolidly, shaking his head.

"There won't be any more orders. Not from there. The bridge is gone."

The rest couldn't hear this above the roar of the inferno; but they could read Ginger's lips, and we were with him. No use staying here.

It was that instant another salvo hit, and the whole side of the *Glorious* seemed to cave in, leaving a choking cloud of smoke and a thunderous roar that echoed away to the darkening sky. The sea, so calm before the action, was now churned up and flecked with ugly grey. God, I thought, we've nearly had our chips. Stupefied, we waited. And I wish we hadn't. For that's when I saw Ginger McColl. He was walking over from his post with P.5. Walking. Holding on to the crazily twisted rails of the ship and laughing at me.

"You're a lucky lot of sods, you are. You're all right. That was our gun, that was. Lifted the whole ruddy gun right out. Last I saw was that bloke Jarvis over with it, looking as if he was holding the gun in his great mitt, like he holds a water-polo ball."

"It got the whole of P.5's crew then?" I said. "Jarvis, and Nutty Almond, too?"

"Yes, Nutty's gone. The whole damn gun-platform just went."

"But you're all right."

"Yes, I'm all right, chum." What a wonderful bloke. His personality could get him out of anything. Nobody quite like Ginger McColl. Even when the whole gun went up, it couldn't give him his chips.

Then I saw why he was walking oddly. His uniform was ragged, what was left of it. Just a torn shirt and part of his trousers. One leg was shot off, and there was the splintered bone, dripping red and black blood, and white strings of sinews. My throat was full of spittle, and I could vomit just to look at him. I thought the world of Ginger.

"I must go and get this wrapped up," was all he said, then hobbled off, guiding his way through the smoke and clutching the twisted rail.

"Let's get," I said, and the rest of our lot followed me, clambering up towards the flight-deck. In the grey steel plating was the shell-hole. The first shell-hole I'd ever seen. Fascinated, I gazed at the jagged edges. A young sailor came screaming down the ladder from the deck, and he was clutching the rails with both hands, kicking out with both feet. I could see he wasn't injured, only hysterical.

"Cut it out," said Taff. "Cut it out, lad."

And he lunged out and hit the kid a welt across the face so hard it sent him staggering back against the deck. The kid stopped screaming all right.

We ran on. There was the hangar, the wall of fire still rising. Struck by the intensity of it all, my mind stopped, and in the eye of memory I could see myself a boy again, in the kitchens of the Queen's, Birmingham.

There's our deep fry, a great oval tray of boiling fat nearly four feet across, smoking on the stove. A fool of a girl scoops out some of the chips we've blanched the day before, then jolts the tray. I scream to her to leave it alone, and grab the pan to stop her. It wobbles. It slips on the bar of the red-hot stove, and the fat spills over into a cascading torrent of fire...

The memory picture faded and there was the hangar, just such another wall of flame. There was nothing we could do here. But the lower hangar? Half a dozen of us ran to the nearest water-tight door, which by war-time routine at sea was always closed. One man alone couldn't undo the great lock. So we all clambered for a hand-hold.

Another swing and we've done it, boys... With our combined weight we heaved, and the door gave. It gave so suddenly we were all flung on our backsides, and the flame gushed out like the very flames of hell. I thought the huge steel door of the hangar would never swing back. It was like the boiler end of an express train coming up at you.

We scrambled up, cursing the fire, cursing the door, shouting to one another for help to get it shut again, as the giant inrush of air gave new zest to the furnace. As tongues of flame shot out, I got to one side of the door with Taff, and as we began to heave it shut there was a sight on the deck such as I could never picture even in a nightmare.

The wheel-lock of that door had huge star-fish spokes. The spokes of that wheel had pinned one of the crew, running right through his body with a clear X pattern like a bruised hot-cross bun. He must have died instantly, the way the imprint of the wheel was left right through his diaphragm. And there was a bit of his shirt, squelching blood, still hanging from the wheel-lock.

I reckon we went berserk at that door. But somehow we got it shut, imprisoned the flames that by now were eating the heart out of *Glorious*, We dripped sweat with the effort and were blackened by the flames. But I still had my jacket on. That was damn silly. So I took it off, and laid it over the punctured corpse on the deck.

By now the *Glorious* was listing, and all the filth was draining that way across the slanting decks.

Through the smoke we could see that P.5 was not the only gun to be lifted clear by shell-fire. We were listing to starboard, and the men could hardly find a footing as they scrambled away from the red-hot and smoking debris. Funny, at that moment I wasn't afraid. I wanted to get on with the thing, as if it was all a game, as if there'd be tea and bread and dripping from the galley when it was over. And everything like it was before. Just twenty minutes before.

Taff and some of the others went off with the Surgeon-Commander, and helped in humping the wounded to the sick-bay. Somebody shoved a handful of glucose sweets into my hand, and they stopped me wanting to vomit.

Then I went back to the gun. The Mangaroo kid was still there, helplessly trying to load it, cursing in his soft Irish way with words I didn't understand.

"Merciful Jaesus where have you been?" he called, startled. "The power's off, and I can't work the rammer."

"I know, kid," I said. "We've been hit below the water-line. All the power's off."

"But I can't work the power rammer," he began to scream.

"Let it be. Let it be," I said. I was too sick and tired to start explaining. Let him scream.

Then the others came back, and he shut up. Well, there was plenty to get on with now, and I'd have pushed the green-eyed newt over the guardrail rather than have him go on screaming. But he shut up.

There we were, standing in the middle of a dozen rounds of ammunition, the projjies all fused. If a Nazi projjie landed in the middle of that lot, we'd be for it.

"Got to get 'em over," said Dully laconically, and just as we were figuring it out, along came one of the sergeants, a good lad called Bentley, and gave us a lead. One of the Marines from another guncrew was there, too, a chap called Steed. If it hadn't been for them, I reckon I would have been too scared to get on with the job. Heaving live projjies overboard isn't funny. I don't know if I was more scared or tired out, and I never wanted to lump another 4.7 again.

Just then we got the order to abandon ship, and kicking our way through the stacks of empty shell-cases which we hadn't time to fling over after the live projjies, we marched off, quite orderly, to our special stations.

And then we marched back.

The Abandon Ship order was cancelled almost as soon as we got it, and we got the Action Stations again.

"What's the old man playing at?" asked Jerry, but with the bridge hit nobody knew. I thought of the kit in my locker, and the tea we wouldn't get, and of the Jewin' job Ginger Woollon and I were due for at 2030 hours, and I didn't want to leave it. I thought of that poor, mutilated body by the lower hangar door, and I didn't want to leave that either. It seemed somehow irreverent.

"There's only one reason, I figure, why the old man's cancelled Abandon Ship," said Taff in his quiet way, like he always did when he wanted to start an argument. "I reckon the Commander's got an idea we can get out of the range of the buggers' guns if we make a run for it. And we can run faster than they can, I reckon, man ..."

But it wasn't like that. The Abandon Ship order came again soon after — not in the precise metallic way of the Tannoy but with one of the officers running along the battery shouting words which on the *Glorious* sounded brutally unreal: "*Abandon ship... All hands prepare to abandon ship...*"

And off we went like sheep, a thin file of bewildered, scorched and oil-scarred men, joining throngs of others struggling against the sharply listing deck until we became a flood of humanity, pressing through the shell debris and the wreckage, running with the ugly current of a crowd towards our appointed stations for Abandon Ship.

We knew where to go. Week after week, in peace-time and in war, we'd practised it. A lot of bull, just to conform to regulations. We'd never need to know...

Week after week we went through the motions, but not through the actions.

That's the part of the deck you'll stand on, but for Christ's sake don't stand on it now when I've just swabbed it down. That's the guy-rope you'll hang on, but don't hang on the blamed thing now, because it's just been painted...

Now the decks were deep in dust and debris, and the new paint scorched as we were ourselves, and we stood there in flocks, sheep-like, wondering what came next after the order Abandon Ship. We'd never been told what came next.

One or two of the lads took the order literally and threw themselves over the rails.

"For God's sake, come back," their pals screamed after them as they dived off the listing deck; but it was no use. The speed we'd been travelling when the action was at its height meant the *Glorious* still had way on her, and to dive into that white frothing cauldron now meant being left miles behind without a hope of rescue.

We felt perplexed because up to this awful moment we'd been obeying orders, and now there weren't any more orders to obey. What comes after Abandon Ship…?

Then it was we saw how wonderful the officers could be. There were the hordes of bruised and injured men waiting like an untidy crowd at the end of a seaside pier, and there was the Major of Marines and two other officers by the hatchway leading down from the centre of the quarterdeck.

"Come on, lads. Don't panic now. Get into line…"

It was nothing they said, really. But the way they stood there and said it. They could have buggered off and left us.

Orders were what we wanted, so they gave us orders. You and you and you. That's right, lads. The three of you. Check the cutter in the storage bay…

We checked it.

In the next bay to where I was standing was storage for a motor-driven cutter, a thirty-foot clinker-built job. Now the planking was jagged and shelled. The transom was split off. The launching cradle was smashed. And, anyway, we could not launch the thing because of the list of the ship. But we checked it, like we'd been told to do.

There were useful, purposeful things to do as well.

There was the job of getting floatable things off that were left undamaged on board. There was the idea of getting some rations in case any of the ship's boats had no fresh stores or water; but this was now too late and impossible. There was the matter of tending to the men who had not been injured seriously enough during the action to be taken to the first-aid posts, but who were now flagging from the strain and shock.

Next to me was a matelot suffering from gun-shock, and he kept on trying to vomit until his frame was weak with retching. Somewhere in my trousers pocket I found the sticky paper of glucose sweets, and he sucked them and gave me a bit of a smile. That stopped it.

By now the quarterdeck was sloping at an angle of nearly forty-five degrees, and as each man prepared to jump, it meant a struggle to climb up for it. Little knots of men clawed each other round the waist as they clambered up to the rails, laughing and swearing as they stripped off their boots and trousers and prepared to jump.

Then my turn came. I got to the top of the deck, and stood there looking down. It must have been thirty feet. And down there I saw the ship's screw on the starboard side still churning beneath me.

It was going to be one hell of a jump. I didn't want to hit that ruddy great green bronze screw, nor any of those oily black bobbing heads in the water.

"Teach you to drown, young 'un!"

A voice was driving through my brain.

It was my brother Bill. We were at New Brighton again, when I was a kid and he was teaching me to swim. Swim? Well, he held me up by the chin, then yelled: "Teach you to drown, young 'un," and he let me go. A couple of mouthfuls, I kicked out. And I could swim. No foot on the bottom. I could really swim.

"Teach you to drown, young 'un..."

That laughing voice followed me as I jumped.

5

THE water was black, and as hard and cold as ice as I hit it.

A scouser, the sea in my blood, there was no moment of fear as I jumped, but I wasn't prepared for the grim violence of the next few minutes. Never in my life had I taken a header for anything deeper than just a plunge off the deep end of the baths; now I was falling in space, spread-eagled.

I hit the surface a belly-flop, then went down like a stone, half unconscious with the Arctic grip of the water after the scorching heat round the gun.

And, like a stone, I sank… Just how far and at what point I began to float upwards I'll never know, for the brutal slam of hitting the water had winded me almost into insensibility. There was a whirling impression of green and black. Then I broke surface and breathed again.

It must have been a couple of minutes at least, after surfacing and trying to tread water, that I realised the intensity of the cold, and the terrific impact with which I must have hit the water.

For one thing, all my shoulders and side were bruised, as though I had fallen on concrete. For another, my long sea-boot stockings had peeled off, in the mighty suction drag as I surfaced after the dive. So I was just in my pants, vest, shirt and trousers, with nothing else to keep out the cold. Undoing the quick-thread stopper, I blew air into my lifebelt, and watched it swell round waist and shoulders.

That was the moment I knew I was facing death for the first time. There had been no such thought in my mind in the action of the preceding two hours of hell.

I had seen my pal with his leg shot off; I had watched the men who had been my shipmates for years vomit to an awful death; I had heard the awful clang of metal as shell-splinters rebounded from the ship's plates a yard or two behind. Even then I had not realised I was looking straight into the face of death.

But now...

It was that M.O.'s lecture we had when we first started the Norway run; that's what was rattling my brain.

"P.T., chaps. Dull stuff and a bit of a bind. But you'll need it now to keep the blood running. These past two and a half years in Mediterranean sunshine have thinned the blood, and for a time your resistance is lowered."

That's why I was always scrambling around the flight-deck to keep my fat down. That's why we ate so many spuds, and scrounged extra sweaters to put on at night when we got into our hammocks, instead of undressing. Thin blood. And now this... a cold so intense it gripped your whole body with a steel hand.

Not that I was afraid to die. I knew I was for it. The only question was: *How long...?*

And how would it happen? How long before I became just a bit of bloody Icelandic cod? What goes first? Is it your heart, or do your legs and arms get numbed while you've still any power left to know and think and feel...?

How long would it take before I stiffened up and the water soaked through my flesh and into my bones? What happened after I became frozen and waterlogged, like an old, rotten tree-trunk? Would this lifebelt keep me supported, bobbing in mock courtesy to the waves and the unchanging Arctic skies, until the flesh had rotted off my bones? Or would I sink through this black, freezing, oily hell into a timeless oblivion?

For maybe ten minutes or more my mind was on these matters, but now time was ceasing to matter. I had all the time there was, until death released me.

And then suddenly the cold acted on the heart like a tonic, and instead of rocking in the oil-scarred brine like a rotting cork, I began to strike out, not only in self-preservation but in anger.

I damned the sea, the Nazis and the war. I damned the *Glorious*, and the blamed fool idea I ever had of enlisting as a dirty-face Marine just because I wanted to show my old man I could make good on my own without a trade. I damned the bloody guns which were outranged in war, and I damned the world that got us into this war. A war that wasn't our fault. Not my fault. Not my fault I was here, drowning.

I hit out and went on hitting out, a cruel, crude, hard-hitting trudgeon stroke which slowly pulled me farther away from the other bobbing heads in this stinking circle of oily water. And the *Glorious*, still with way on her though her engines were crippled, was well away over there, no more than an ugly wreck on the skyline.

Around me were probably nearly fifteen hundred others, yet I felt alone, terribly alone.

The more I saw of the others, the more I realised the intensity of my loneliness. For some of them were dead already.

Some were almost non-swimmers, and the shock of the deep dive had been fatal. They knew they were jumping to their certain death, poor devils, but they jumped unflinchingly because they got the order. The order Abandon Ship.

Now the ship had abandoned them. And they were dead, gripped in their lifebelts, bobbing like a mute chorus of flotsam.

Christ, I said, that's not going to be me. That's not the way I'm going. And I'm not going now. I'm not prepared for it. I don't know what death is. I don't know what you have to do when you die.

That was the moment when I ought to have said a prayer, but I hadn't said a real prayer since I was eight or nine, and there weren't any words to be mustered now, so I swam on desperately. Not afraid to die. But afraid of a strange new life called death, and of which I knew nothing. I struck out angrily.

Within the next few minutes, frog-leg kicking up out of the water now and then to give my arms a rest and so that I could see above the debris, the flotsam and the floating heads, I spotted a cushion. It must have been one of the air-cushions from a lifeboat. Four other men saw it about the same time. Three of them reached it with me. We didn't see the fourth again.

Would it hold the four of us? If not, who would let go?

We clung there, brushing the oil from our eyes, panting for breath, staring at each other with bloodshot eyes.

For a while we didn't want to speak. We had to save our breath. Who they were, I don't know. On a ship the size of the *Glorious* there are a good many you never know, and, anyway, it's only your own messmates who mean anything. The others at times you could hate as much as if they were in the Nazi Navy, such is the unreal driving force of Service rivalries and petty loyalties. But now these men, these three and I, were united in staring at the face of a stranger called death.

And in the face of death, what did we say?

"God, this is a proper do and no mistake," said one.

"If we can keep going like this, we'll make it," said another.

And a third asked anxiously: "Think there's a chance we'll get picked up by our own lot, before the Jerries get to us...?"

I was the one who stayed silent, because in my heart I didn't think there was a chance we'd get picked up by our lot, or by Jerry either. But I thought if we kept going like this we might just make it. And silently I was telling God this is a proper do and no mistake

"How can you stop the cold getting you?" one asked. And then we all started, gasping out fantastic ideas for bending your knees, or kicking out of the water, or anything that might keep the blood running, and ward off the vicious grip of frostbite. But we hadn't the strength to demonstrate what we were talking about, and after a bit we had no wish to talk about it either.

We clung to that canvas cushion, staring at the waves, staring at each other. One of the men began to retch, and there was nothing we could do to stop the vomit spewing all round us on the greasy oil. He wiped his eyes and said he was sorry, but it was the seasickness. And the rest of us just grunted and clung there.

No wonder he was seasick. I hadn't realised it until now. This lovely June afternoon had been cut up by the gunfire, and as the smoke-screen of the ill-fated destroyers trailed away, it left an angry, grey sea, mountain-tossed with the devil-made storm. No wonder this perisher was retching his heart up.

When he stopped, he was very white, the pallor heightened by the black streaks of his lank, oil-soaked hair, his neck tacky with the yellow vomit. For a time he lay there, bobbing up and down, one white, steel-like claw clenched to the cushion. But a tall wave took him off, and none of us had the strength to grab him.

We didn't look each other in the eyes, and it was a long time before I spat the water out of my mouth and said: "Poor sod. I reckon one of the boats'll pick him up."

"Aye, I reckon," said one of the other men around the cushion.

But I didn't like to look him in the face, because I knew that he could have reached out a hand and perhaps saved this poor vomiting bastard from certain death. And I knew he was thinking the same about me. So I looked away, at the sea around us.

That's when I saw what I thought was a raft or maybe a Carley float, and momentarily I was so overjoyed that I choked and the words would not come. But I managed to point, and one of the men on the cushion strained high on the edge of it, and smiled through the oil streaks, asking: "Think we can make it, chum?"

We tried. But after a few yards I realised I was the only one swimming. The others already had cramp and could not move their limbs. Looking back, I saw that this fierce spurt of energy had driven the grin from the face of this man who'd urged me to try; and now he was just being pulled along with the cushion. So I struck out even harder in a sort of mad frenzy with one hand, trying to drag the air-cushion with the two men clutching it.

Obviously this was impossible. It was one long, futile struggle with the waves, making no progress against them.

So I let the cushion go …

Would they die? Anyway, why should I die? It wasn't my bloody war. If I clung to the cushion with the rest of them, we'd all go. That was certain. But if I struck out in time, maybe I could just make that float. Then at least one of us would be safe. Could I help it if that one was me? It wasn't my bloody war. Why should I have to make all the decisions?

The distance was only about fifty yards. It seemed like fifty miles. My strokes became weaker and weaker as the cold bit deeper, and I knew it would be impossible to carry on much longer.

Then I heard a voice I knew. "*Wotcher, Tubby! Trying to swim home?*" it said.

I managed to raise my head from the foamy, black water, and break the subconscious rhythm of my trudgeon stroke, and saw that it was Nobby Clark, a fellow Marine, the one who always made me laugh because he loved chewing wads of india-rubber as a change from ship's plug. It was Nobby who, along with Sticks Bevis, my fellow signalman Percy Padwick and Wally Goodenough were in so many flunks' scrapes with me. Now Nobby was clinging to an oar, pathetically happy in his plight, yelling out: *"Trying to swim home?"*

Not having the strength to call back, I grinned, and he grinned again at me. And strength seemed to flow into my arms.

I kicked out the last fifteen yards or so, and reached my objective. It was not a Carley float, but one of the motor-boats from the *Glorious*, badly damaged and well down in the water. At first I thought she was filled almost to the gunwales, but then I realised that the stern was only covered in spray, and one more body aboard would not be too much. I trod water for a minute or two, striving to summon enough strength to pull myself over the side. There was nobody looking over the stem or stern, and she just rode there in the grey seas like an ill-fated vessel of doom.

But as I pulled myself up and over and strong arms came out to help me, I saw there were about twenty men aboard. Who they were, I did not care. That we might all thus die together left me unmoved. That last fifty yards had been covered, and now I was safe, at least for a time.

So there I lay, almost rigid with cold, my shirt oil-soaked and scraping my flesh, my eyes burning with the brine and oil so all I wanted to do was close them and sleep.

It was a song which woke me. No telling how long I'd been asleep. They were singing "Roll Out the Barrel." If you could call it singing. These were men whose throats were parched with sea-water; dazed from shock and exposure.

"*Roll out the barrel*," they were singing,
"*Let's have a barrel of fun…*"

One chap I knew, a Marine corporal, was sitting in the fore part of the motor-boat beating time with his left hand, hanging on to the ratline with the other. His choir of freezing, drenched mortals, who were a handful of Hitler's prey and quarry, were singing with cracked and parched voices:

"*Roll out the barrel,*
We've got the Hun on the run…"

They quavered to silence, but one man went on muttering: "… and be of good cheer. So roll out the bloody barrel, for the gang's all here…"

"*The gang's all here.*" His croak rose to a sort of climax.

I looked around at the gang.

"Good lad, Tubby," said the corporal. "Glad you were able to make it."

You'd think he was offering an invitation to a beer party. The gang. Yes, there were about twenty in the boat. I didn't count them. I never did count them. My glance naturally flashed first to those I knew… to Tim Healy, the sergeant of flunks, to the Marine corporal, to the Surgeon-Commander, and the Surgeon-Lieutenant (D).

Not having exhausted themselves swimming in the Arctic water, their strength was not sapped as mine was, and for a long time I lay there just watching, and thinking, and listening.

They had lashed themselves with rope to avoid being carried away by the heavy seas which were now breaking over us, and after a few minutes I thought it wiser to copy their example and one of the officers helped me to hitch the line. He pulled it very tight.

"That's a bit too much, sir," I said. "Bit too tight, I mean. Don't you think it ought to be left slack, sir?"

It was damn silly "sir-ing" a man in this predicament, but, after all, he was an officer.

"Better have it tight," he said. "Stops the chafing."

"O.K.," I said. And I didn't add "sir." I thought it was daft to pull the rope tight, but I was too weak to belly-ache about it right then.

After another hour or so two of the Marine "bandies" started another sing-song, with Corporal Jagger leading. And while they were singing I managed to unhitch the rope and allow enough slack to keep me on top of each wave.

The truth was that as the waves struck the boat it didn't rise and fall very much, being so waterlogged. But human bodies rose and fell with the waves, and those who were roped too tightly together were put to unnecessary strain. Well, that's how it seemed to me. The officer who'd helped me hitch myself just watched silently, so I said: "I feel a bit more comfortable like that, sir."

He waved assent. And something made me add: "I hope you don't mind."

Mind! As if it was his damned boat. He was lucky to be there, just as I was. But he was a good chap, and he meant well by the tight-hitching.

I had the impulse to go on, to say: Why don't you let me give you enough slack so you ride the waves, sir? Then it won't take the guts out of you each time the sea grabs your water-soaked body and flings it against the gunwale and planking, sir. But I didn't.

"*We're going to hang out the washing on the Siegfried Line*," they were singing, and a score of heads, rocked by the boat, were trying to wag in time with the song.

I found myself in chorus, but the words wouldn't come and I was too tired to think of them, so I just "da-da-dee-da'd" it. And then we sang "*Bless 'em all*." And when it came to the crappy bits about the officers and the W.O.s, the Surgeon-Commander was joining in, and trying to laugh in a funny cracked sort of way. Anyway, his eyes were laughing, and he kept pushing his oil-matted hair away from his forehead, and our eyes met.

I wasn't looking at this briny, oil-smeared, dishevelled figure. I was looking at the spruce Surgeon-Commander I always knew on the *Glorious*, the one for whom my special pal Bill Hutchings was flunk — Bill, the one who was always letter-writing, even on defence stations around the gun. Bill, the one who almost worshipped the ground his officer walked on, and who said he was the best doc, and the best officer, and the best man, he ever wanted to team up with.

And I was thinking of the dozen and one little incidents in the happy family of the *Glorious*. Of that sun-drenched Aden and Mediterranean cruising life when the great grey hull of the *Glorious* rode like a proud mountain from the sunlit blue, when the Surgeon-Commander leaned over the rails yelling louder than anyone else when it was little dark blue-eyed Mickie Bolan. I was seeing not this disordered, scarred wreck of a man, but the officer other men loved. And here he was singing in that funny croaking voice with the others; in our Arctic plight:

> *"Sod'em all!*
> *Sod'em all!*
> *The long and the short and the tall..."*

When they had finished singing, I half rolled myself along the carvel planking until I was lying next to Tim Healy, the sergeant of flunks. Somehow I felt I wanted to be near him, to talk to somebody I knew, and to help him if that was still possible. He was lying there very quiet. Well, he hadn't got my fat. Fat — the fat of your own belly — is far better for keeping out the cold than any home-knitted comforts.

I thought he was asleep, but I touched his thigh as the next wave came and I struggled to hitch myself to his part of the rope, and he opened his eyes and gave me a smile. Such a funny smile it was: funny coming from him, I mean. For a moment it made him seem a real stranger. Healy was a typical sergeant of flunks, stiff as starch, straight and strict, and I reckon I'd hardly ever seen him smile. Perhaps that was it.

Yet, when he smiled there was the answer to the whole enigma. Through his smiling eyes I could see a man with a great heart, a sergeant so loyal to the lads around him that if an officer ever belly-ached about one of us, Healy would rear up, go red in the neck and answer back: "Well, sir, fair's fair. The man can't do your work and also be at defence stations round a gun." But as soon as the officer had passed on, Healy would give you a proper rocket and leave you thinking: "Well, he was a good sort. He smoothed it over, and didn't bawl you out in front of an officer." A thousand little loyalties like that make you respect a man.

"How're you doing, Tubby?" he asked. I never even knew he heard that's what the boys called me.

"Not bad. Not bad at all, Sarge." I smiled. "It's having it here, round the belly, that helps. But I could do with a drop of kye, and I reckon you could too."

"If I had the key to the rum barricoe, I'd drink the ruddy lot," he said with a grin. "Unless you beat me to it, sonny."

"Well, there's no keyboard sentry here, Sarge," I said.

"And there's no ruddy rum either," he said. "But we'll enjoy it all the better when we get it."

When…

With a couple of the other Marines, Healy and I tried to play tombola with words. Healy was that sort. Nights in the *Glorious*, after watch and after all my Jewin' jobs, I'd get back to find the sergeant was playing tombola with the boys, just like one of us. Well, now we hadn't any cards. But we could go through the motions, and somehow it helped doing familiar things, saying the things you know to the men you know. Imagining we'd got our fifteen numbers… imagining…

The worst of it was we had no idea of the time. You can stand a pain or a thirst for ten minutes, or maybe half an hour, or an hour. But when minute runs into minute, hour into hour, and night continuously into day, the strain becomes unbearable. In these latitudes there is almost no difference between night and day, and we had no idea how long we'd been in the boat. Because there was no night I could not sleep. I was too exhausted to sleep.

After what seemed a lifetime, just lying there on my ratline, listening to the thud of bodies against the planking and the rush of the dark water, I was suddenly alarmed by the noise of a scrimmage. One man, crazed with thirst or exhaustion, had started to attack his neighbour on the ratline, and was striking at him all round. A proper ding-dong it was, and those of us near to the struggling couple were too weak to drag them apart. The crazy one had gained an almost superhuman strength.

Who it was, I don't know, but somebody stood poised by the breast-hook, then brought both hands down with one of the boat fittings on the skull of the man who had gone berserk, and there was quiet. All of a sudden, he went rigid. And that's how he lay. I didn't like to look.

What good is a crazed man in a small boat, along with twenty others? What good is a crazed man who'll be dead in twelve hours anyway?

"Will one or two of you help me to get him over the side?"

It was the Surgeon-Commander. We freed ourselves enough on our ratlines to be able to heave the body over.

The man who'd hit him said nothing, but just sat there crying, his whole frame shaking with great sobs; and as the body was rolled over the side he hid his face with his oily hands. Hansen, the other Marine bandie, began to sing to take his mind off it all.

"*Roll out the barrel,*" he croaked. "*Let's have a barrel of fun...*"

The crudity, the sheer godless crudity of our plight was too much for me. "*Roll out the barrel.*" I began to laugh, a laugh which rolled out into one long hysterical scream, and I knew they were looking at me but I didn't give a damn.

6

I DIDN'T sleep at all in the boat, but there were times when I was either stretched out over the coaming or standing up by the quarter-knees to alleviate the grating pain of my frost-bitten legs, when mind seemed separated from body. And although my eyes were opened to the sky and sea, I saw nothing.

When I turned and looked inboard again, Healy was dead.

There was no doubt about it. Nobody seemed to know but me. I crawled on my knees, unhitching my ratline, then stood there over Healy, looking down at the grey-white oil-scarred travesty of the man I had loved and feared and hated; and now at the eleventh hour when I had seen him smile I had seen his soul. I thanked Providence for that.

"All right," I said. "I can manage." They wanted to help me, and the Surgeon-Commander struggled to his feet and with outstretched arms motioned the others back as I stooped to pick the body up and rolled it over the gunwale.

Then I collapsed into my place, and sat silent, heavy at heart.

This awful finality of death was something I could not bear, and in some odd fashion I felt responsible for Healy. True, I wasn't sleeping, but maybe if I had been looking I would have known how he was suffering.

Perhaps if I had been able to punch him into sensibility, or to massage his heart, or clutch him with the failing warmth of my own body...

That his lifestream should have slipped away while I was not even looking filled me with self-reproach.

Not that I was afraid of facing death. There was that grey-white face, so hard and solid in its death-mask, just as had been the first death-mask I ever saw. That was a long time ago. Another life, another age ago: when I was a kid of nine.

A school-mate and I were running from school, out of the gates and across the park, and because I was tubby even then my stumpy legs wouldn't keep up, he was several paces ahead of me. So he came on it first — the cruel sight of another of our school children, mown down by a fire engine, which killed him and roared on without stopping.

We looked, and saw the crumpled, distorted body — a child's body, but with the hard, firm mask of death just as I had now seen on Healy.

I ran a mile and kept on running as if I could run away from this afflicting sight. It was dark when I plucked up courage to go home, and Dad was back from work. I was afraid to go home — afraid because in some queer way I felt to blame; afraid of what might have happened if that mutilated body had been mine. Afraid...

Then memory took me on some years to when my little cousin Peggy fell from a window, right on her face, and the doctors patched her crumpled body so that she lived five years more, then died of pneumonia. I saw her in her coffin, with that same fixed mask, the mask the Creator leaves on us in place of the lovely face of life. It was the same in the boat ...

Two or three died, and we accepted their passing as inevitable. But was it? I got talking to the Surgeon-Commander.

"What're our chances, do you reckon, sir?" I asked.

He raised himself weakly from his corner by the quarter-knees and laughed softly. "I was just trying to work that one out for myself, son. As I see it, the facts aren't very pleasant either. Not the sort of things you like thinking of, let alone telling to any other man."

"Tell it to the Marines," I said.

"Well, you've seen three of us die. And at my reckoning we've been in this boat six hours. Maybe seven. What do you think our chances are for the rest?"

"Me? I don't know. I only know that when they gave us the Abandon Ship order and I dived off, I figured I was going to die in half an hour. Thought the cold would get me, or the oily water would drag me down, or that I wouldn't be able to reach anything to float on... But I didn't die, though I saw others who did. I'm not afraid of death. But I just want to know. *I want to know.* That's all!"

And I shut up quick, because I realised I was shouting. And it tires you when you shout.

"Well, son," he said quite quietly. "The way I figure it is this. It's a gamble. A race, if you like. On the one side there's the exposure, the fact that we can't get any shelter, or warmth, or fresh water to drink. Whatever stores there were in this confounded boat — if ever there were any —

were shell-blasted out of it before we found her. On the other hand, there's the equal certainty that a signal got through during the action. They wouldn't have kept radio silence all the time. No point in it, after we knew we were outranged, I imagine. The Hun might have got that signal; pretty certain, in fact. They'd be scouring all our frequency bands during an action. So the first possibility is that we might win the gamble against endurance and thirst, and be picked up."

"By…?"

"Precisely. By some antique kite of Coastal Command? Or by a Dornier operating within a hundred miles or less of her base? From what I deduce the chances of our being prisoners of war is about fifty to one… if we're picked up at all."

"Prisoners of war? I reckon they'd just shoot us straight."

"No. They'd figure what we might be able to tell them would be too valuable."

"For you, maybe. But not for an old sweat. Not for a dirty-faced leatherneck Marine."

"Anybody who can talk would be valuable."

"But I don't know anything. I was a flunk. And I was round my gun. I reckon they knew we only had four-point-sevens…"

There was something in his gaze which made me stop. He was not looking in my face, but just over my right shoulder, and I turned to see what it was. There was a man, one of the matelots, crouching by the gunwales, clutching the beam weakly and raising himself a little as if he was about to vomit. Then I saw that he was demented and, with his back towards us was urinating, cupping his hand and wetting his lips.

"For Christ's sake stop that fool," gasped the Surgeon-Commander weakly, and I mustered strength and lunged out at him so that he stumbled in the act and collapsed along by the gunwales, where he lay blubbering.

"It's okay," he whimpered. "It's okay if you drink sea-water at the same time. I was only wetting my lips with it…"

"God, you bloody fool," I hissed, angry because until this moment the pangs of thirst had not been unbearable, but now this urinating idiot had opened the floodgates of temptation.

I left him lying there, and crawled back to my position with the Surgeon-Commander.

"What's the answer to it, doc?" I asked softly. "Is it poison? Does it drive you mad?"

"It's all right, son," he laughed, as if talking to a child. "They say you don't do it — don't drink your own, I mean — until it's almost too late to matter. That's what's worrying me… not for myself, I mean, but for some of the others who didn't get on this bloody boat until they were shell-shocked and worn out. They started with such low vitality that now—"

He trailed away into silence.

"Tell me straight, doc," I asked. "For myself, I mean. I'm tubby. I'm bloody cold, but there's still plenty of fat on me, and it hasn't chilled my bones yet. But I'm no superman, and I just want to know. How much longer can a man go without water?"

"Another day maybe. It all depends what other demands there are on the system."

"We ought to just lie quiet and not move or talk."

"Then we'll become frozen cod. No, we've got to keep active so the circulation is normal. Once you get in a coma, it's dangerous, believe me. That's why you've seen me punching some of the chaps to keep them awake."

"But you didn't answer my question, doc. Can you drink your own and get away with it? Is it possible to drink it, I mean?"

"After ship's cocoa, you can drink anything, son. Forget it. It won't kill you. But it won't save your life. We've got worse things to face than that..."

Hour in, hour out, we just rocked and lay there, chafing in the ropes we'd harnessed to ourselves, but I was now so cold and numb the ropes hardly hurt. They were like steel bands; but my frozen arms were also steel, and feeling was almost gone. What worried me most was my tongue, which was beginning to swell with the salt; and my face, too, felt blistered and swollen.

Then I began to get worried about the three or four others for whom I could do nothing; one obviously in great abdominal pain and who gave vent to crudities which brought tears to my salt-rimmed eyes; the others were moaning to themselves, bent and lying in an attitude of resignation.

A few more hours and it was all up for them. Well, I didn't know them, and there was nothing I could do. But the Surgeon-Commander was watching them, and as they died I saw his expression take on the unforgettable appearance of utter despair. He stared at me blankly, with eyes filled with tears that would not come.

We were heartbroken, watching men die and powerless to save them.

My lips and tongue were sore, and I could speak only in whispers, but I wanted to ask so many questions. If this was how it was going to end, there was so much I must yet know. So much he might be able to tell me to help for my own fate ahead, in perhaps an hour or two at the most.

"Can — can you talk?" I asked, and he weakly smiled assent.

"I'm puzzled," I said. "Why does God let it happen?"

"You mean all this suffering — and death?"

"Yes, if God made the world — and all that sort of cock we were taught at school — if he made everything and people — and Hitler and you and me. Well, why does he let it happen? Men being shelled to pieces and drowned, I mean. Why doesn't he stop it?"

The Surgeon-Commander didn't answer for a minute.

"What are you asking me that one for, Tubby? I'm the doctor, not the padre."

"I know, I know. But you're the only man I can ask, and I've got to know. If I'm going to die in an hour or so, I've got to know what sort of dam' God I'm going to meet. If he won't even lift his little finger to stop us freezing to death or dying of thirst, I don't know as I'm so bloody keen to meet him. Why doesn't he stop it?"

"Because he can't."

"For Christ's sake, what do you mean *'Because he can't?'*"

"I'm telling you. It's just as simple as that."

"But he made you and me, and the sea, the *Glorious*, the guns, and fifty million bloody Nazis. What are we, then? Just pawns on a chessboard? Numbers in a game of tombola?"

"Listen, son," said the Surgeon-Commander, after I'd let him wait a minute to gather his strength. "You've left it darned late in life to start asking bloody silly questions about your Creator, but if you want to know the answer to it all, I'll tell you. And, mind you, I'm only telling you what I figure is the answer. If we get out of this, you can start figuring it out for yourself. Have you ever heard of the conservation of energy?"

"Like bloody hell I have."

"Well, it means that all the energy in the world goes round and round in some way or another, and never gets wasted. No more comes in and none goes out. This sea-water, for instance. It gets drawn up into the clouds as vapour by the sun, then comes down as rain again, and gets back to the sea through the streams and rivers. Everything's like that; in the physical world anyway."

"And so?"

"Well, the scientists have got it all wrapped up nicely, except for one thing.

"Their theories don't take into account any of the things you and I are interested in — not the things of the mind, or of what the padre calls the spirit. Love, hate, lusting after anybody, or doing good. Those don't come into the conservation of energy plan at all.

"And you know why? Because these are the things that belong to God. When we die now, our bodies go over the gunwales, and rot in the ocean and decay. That's all part of the conservation of energy theory. But our spirit is quite a different sort of thing, and that's free and goes back to God."

"But I still don't see why God can't stop the guns that murder us or the sea that chokes us."

"Because he didn't make them and he can't stop them."

"That's crazy."

"Is it?"

"Yes, God made everything and everybody."

"I don't believe that. Nor do many others. If you believe that, the problem is incapable of solution. You only go on knocking your head against a wall. No, the way I figure it out is this. The universe, the world, everything: God didn't make them. Not what we understand by 'God,' anyway.

"Life in various forms was evoked out of the Earth, but at some time in the world's history a loving spirit called God brought mankind into it, to work out a big purpose. He works his plan and uses the ordinary material things of this universe, but he didn't create them and he is powerless to stop them hurting if we use them wrongly."

"I don't get it," I said.

"Don't worry your head about it," he said. "I told you, you've left it rather late to find out. Most people do. I can't make it clear to you now. I'd talk easier if I had my pipe on and a good double tot."

"I'll look forward to having it with you, sir," I said.

"Do that, Tubby," he said, and relapsed into silence.

I lay there thinking. I grasped his idea. People and all the warm and kind things, the passionate and lustful things; the things you can't touch or weigh in a balance. Yes, those are the things of the spirit. And the cruel sea, the steel-like ropes and the biting brine. These are the things of the material world, which God did not make and through which he tries to steer our spirit.

"Does he do it because he loves us, or because there's Hell if we don't do the right thing?"

He looked at me, comprehending the question.

"Because of love. God is love. There isn't any Devil. Everything cruel and evil is turning away from God, like turning away from the sunshine to the shade. That's all."

"I see..." But I didn't. One mighty obstacle arose.

"The whole thing's nuts," I said, "if you don't mind my saying so. If God didn't make the world, who did?"

"Nobody," he croaked. "Physical things have always existed and always will. That's what they mean by the conservation of energy."

"Conservation my backside," I said. "It's too puzzling. I don't find it any comfort."

"You will. We'll talk about it another time, but I've got the cramp in my thighs so badly I can't think. Give me a thump if I look like going off to sleep, there's a good chap. Mustn't go off to sleep..."

It was about two hours after that, I should imagine, when he stirred again. By now the only way in which I could judge time was by apportioning it in my mind's eye as I did when doing my chores in the *Glorious*. Ten minutes to cut a head. An hour under the Malt's eye in the wardroom. Two hours on Defence Stations…

I tried to interpret that now, just laying here with the boat rocking in the lonely Arctic waste, as if I still had these chores to do. And, God, I was parched.

There were now five of us alive. The Surgeon-Commander, a young Marine and three flat-foots. I didn't know the others, and somehow felt drawn by the great personal magnetism of the doc. He beckoned me over with a weak smile. Now his voice was little more than a whisper.

"Look, son," he said, "I'll be the next to go. But because of your build you're going to stick it out. Don't worry. I just don't feel able to get to my feet. I've been trying for the last half-hour or so. But I want you to take a vow. I want you to cut those chaps loose when their time comes. It will help you to last longer. And do the same for me when my time comes."

"That's just bloody murder," I said. "Anyway, I haven't a knife."

I turned away to sea, anxiously scanning the wheel of the horizon, wondering if my eyes would be closed with the agony of the salt by the time help came near. And I'd be blind and unable to call for help…?

My heart throbbed and fretted on this anxiety for hours maybe. And when I looked around again, one of the men was wearing that familiar hard mask of death, and the companion roped near him was weakly signalling me to free the rope. I groped in his pocket and found the hard outline of a knife.

"Good lad," croaked the doc feebly when I had cut them free, and I turned in a frenzy.

What a fool. What a stark, crazy fool. I had been daydreaming, not protecting the doc as I should, and there he was lying near the quarter-knees, sunk down below the oak crooks with his head at an ugly angle. I flung myself on him and clutched him as if he was a woman, to give him the feeble warmth of my body. I pummelled him and nestled him to give him life. But it was too late, and I knew I was grasping a dead man.

The boat was rocking badly, or perhaps it was because I was now so weak. A wave dashed him over the gunwale as I released my grip, and he hung there by the ratline wrapped around his wrists. I cut him loose, and watched horror-struck as he sank slowly behind the transom of the boat.

What prayer could I offer? "God take him," I whispered. "He said it was like turning away from the shade to the sunshine. He's turned to you, God. Take good care of him, God."

A child could have done better, and I could have done better — as a child. Since then I'd forgotten how to pray.

I looked around the boat, at the loose ends of the ratlines, where twenty men had sat roped together in grim comradeship, singing:

"Roll out the barrel,
Let's have a barrel of fun..."

Now there was nothing but sea and cold silence. I was alone.

7

I'D never been quite alone before in my life, not even for an hour.

We were a large family, as children. There was Clara and Bill, Anne, Walter. Then me. Clara being older by far than the rest, she mothered us; so there was always somebody around to look after the family even when Mum was out. No, I'd never been alone, not even in the fastnesses of the mind. There'd always been people around me to make up my mind for me, people to laugh along with, people to grouse at.

The enormity of my present plight did not dawn on me at first. Like one demented, I clambered to the fore part of the boat, grasped the ratlines as if they were reins, and stood there hour after hour imagining I was piloting a chariot through the waves. Yes, I got a kick out of standing up there, facing the spray, fighting back that grating, binding agony in my legs and swearing to God that I was skipper and crew in this bloody boat.

I'm the one that gives the orders. D'you hear? I'm the one that gives the orders. No Captain Bloody D'Oyly Hughes. No goddam Major of Marines. No sweaty, squit-eyed, greasy, crap-livered bastard son of a Maltese Guiseppe. No, sir. I'm the one who gives the orders in this ship.

Or am I going mad…?

Then, for the first time I burst into tears. I'd wanted to cry when I saw Healy and the doc and some of the others die. I'd wanted to cry with horror when I saw men dying in the midst of their own foulness. But the tears would not come into my salt-choked eyes.

Now they did, and I was glad. After my brief moment of pride I felt humble, and I was glad. No, I wasn't the skipper in this boat. I wasn't even the captain of the coming hour or of the coming minutes. I was alone on the uncharted ocean of fate; a grim, awful, unchangeable Fate.

A constricting terror began to grasp my limbs, and I fell deeper into the grip of an insane fear. The brine stung, the charred sea-oil burned my skin, my tongue and lips were swelling with thirst, and the water-logged boat bounded and bumped and swung itself through the waves, pounding my very bones against the boat's planking.

These were the physical things, the things the doc said God didn't create and couldn't control. But the agony in my mind, the awful fear; these were the things of the spirit, the things which hurt and tormented and racked me because I was looking away from God into the darkening shadows. I covered my eyes with swollen hands and tried not so much to pray — because I didn't know the words in my sick confused brain — but to figure it out: to talk to God.

When I opened my eyes, a pale golden sun was shining out of the Arctic sky, and I guessed I'd come through one more night and now it was morning; if my reckoning was right, the morning of the second day.

I went back and clambered again to the bows, holding the rope as I had done before, but now the disorder was passed and the fever cooled, and no longer did I get a kick out of standing there surf-riding.

No longer was I afraid, and as I gazed out to sea I suddenly realised there was still a considerable amount of flotsam, and therefore it must all be drifting from the wrecked carrier in the same direction — perhaps spread out by fifty miles or more. I pondered on the question of the Gulf Stream.

Were we — all these myriad bits of wreck and flotsam — lucky enough to be in the powerful stream, which might circle us round to Greenland, or perhaps even to the fishing-lanes off Scapa?

If this was so, and it seemed reasonable, then there would be a good chance of survival if only I could get out of this water-logged, shell-damaged craft and find something which could give more protection. Food and water were obviously impossible. But if I could conserve my strength, as the doc suggested, I might last in wakefulness or even in a coma for several days, and if all the floating debris stayed in the same ocean current this still might mean survival.

As though by a miracle, I saw on the horizon, about a mile away, two dots. I had to stare at them for minutes, then close my bruised eyes, then stare again, before I could be certain what I was seeing. They were undoubtedly Carley floats.

In half an hour we had drifted closer and I was sure I could see men.

I felt I knew which floats they were. *My* floats: the two Carleys which had stood up on the superstructure of the *Glorious*, near the *Explicit Nomen* motto in brass letters. Many an afternoon in the Mediterranean I'd taken a cat-nap in one of those canvas-covered Carleys, resting my dozing head against the ratlines, loops and toggles. Now the floats were filled with men, probably ninety or so in each.

It took a long time to make up my mind. I dragged the soaked and crumpled photos from my belt — the picture of Mum and Dad on New Brighton beach, and the picture I'd taken of Peg soon after Jim Agnew and I had met up with the girls on the Clarence Pier in Pompey. If there was ever to be a chance of seeing and talking with them all again, I'd got to do something, no matter how big the gamble.

Looking out over the gunwale again, I figured the nearer of the Carleys was now about a mile away, or maybe a little less. But could I swim that far? And if I did start out, would I be able to keep track of the right direction once I was down in the water half hidden from my objective by the tall waves? Then, staring out once again, I saw men move, and the sight of living human beings in that waste of water did something to me. On an impulse I decided to try to reach them.

I deflated my lifebelt, so that if cramp overcame me or the exhaustion was too much to bear, I shouldn't linger but would go straight down. Then I cut myself loose and dropped over the side.

I picked a small patch in the sky as a guide for direction, and struck out through the waves. It was heartening to realise I was making progress. It was the first progressive, active thing I'd done for maybe two days.

Hours it seemed I was swimming. My legs began to grow stiff, first at the feet, then the calves, the knees, the thighs. My stomach became knotted with an intolerable pain, and I knew, as I rose and fell in the waves, that my time had come.

What made me certain was not the agonising pain in my belly, but the fact that now reality had ceased, and images were drifting through my brain, obscuring the green-grey waves ahead. When you're drowning, I'd always been taught, you see your whole past life spread out before you. And it was happening to me. Now.

There I was, back home on leave in Liverpool, in our own little brown sitting-room, with Peg's photo in a frame on the sideboard, and Mum was saying: "Well, Ron, it's about time you made your mind up, after going around with Mabel all these years."

And Peg was on the bus with me, nudging me soft and warm, and saying in those last few moments before I met her family for the first time: "By the way, darling, my name's not Peggy. It's Norah."

"That's what I always reckoned," I said. "And my name's not Christopher Carl Healiss either. It's Ron." Then I flung my arms round her, even though it was a busful of people, and I whispered softly: "God, you're a kind and lovely thing…"

There were less pleasant pictures in my mind. There were the dirty grey-steel kitchens of the swank hotels, the drab background to all the cream-and-gold finery in front There was the recruiting sergeant in Canning Place kidding me with a lot of exciting pictures of foreign places I'd see if I signed on, and as I'd worked with foreigners so much in the hotel kitchens I was a proper sucker for it. He didn't say there were foreigners like Josie the Malt in the Navy… There was the ugly scene when my dad heard I'd signed on — Dad who'd always been trying to plan my career; but as he was trained as a first-class boot- and shoe-maker and I was trained as nothing, Dad's plans didn't come to much. And there was now in my mind the vivid picture of his face when I told him I'd signed on with the Royals, and the letter arrived next day ordering me to report at 0830 with a toothbrush, pants and vest… And Dad said: "Well, that's that, you young fool. You've chucked your life away. You've made your bed, now you must lie on it…"

There was the bitter disappointment when I was sick and fed up with the Marines after the first three hours, with the awful realisation I was in for life. And Dad's kind letter which said: "As you know, son, I was an R.A.S.C. driver in the first war, and that wasn't any fun either. But you've made your bed, son, so make a good soldier. God bless you…"

The passing scenes speeded up, like pages of a book skimmed over.

Norah, warm and scented and kind-eyed, hugging me tight as we kiss good-bye... Serving in *Leander*, and in *Carlisle* for the Spithead Review... Faces, familiar faces passing before me. Voices, familiar voices. These are the people I've known and loved...

I struck out again with fresh strength. Then a wave lifted me, and as I floundered on top of it I saw to my amazement that the two rafts were hardly twenty yards away, and instinctively I struggled towards one. Somebody shouted and I swam towards the voice...

There seemed to be about fifty men, some actually in the Carley, others hanging to the ratlines running in loops around the framework.

I grabbed one of those lines, then looked at the man hanging on the ratline next to me.

"Hello, chum," I said. "Don't look scared. I haven't swum all the way from the *Glorious*, I've been on a water-logged picket-boat all last night..."

He stared at me and I stared back.

His face was deadly white, his lips black.

"Stop staring, you bastard," I was saying to myself, but then I realised why he stared with that glassy expression. The chap was dead, hanging here on the ratline beside me.

I turned my back to shut out the sight of those eyes. The man on the other side of me, also clinging to the ratline, was coughing deeply, a deep choking cough. He couldn't speak, and at every wave he swallowed more water.

I tried to raise his head above the waves, with the help of someone in the float who leant over and grasped his shoulders with oil-stained hands. But his arm was locked in the lifeline, and we couldn't drag him up. We had to let him go, unable to support the dead weight any longer. I was now hanging there between two dead men.

"God, is this what you gave me strength for?" I blubbered. "Why didn't you let me die alone in the boat, along with the others...?"

The frenzy passed. I lifted my swollen face and tried to climb into the float. They helped me up and over, and I lay there for a time, vomiting much of the sea-water I had swallowed in the past hour. And when that attack was over, and I'd flushed my face clean with cupped hands in the water, I felt better.

It was warming to see that the man who'd helped me in to the float was the Signal Bo'sun, a Chiefie with whom I did many a spell of bunting-tossing. Now he was squatting in the float, his chest and hair heavily matted in oil and brine, one arm black with congealed blood from an untended wound.

He gazed at me, then grinned.

"You've been swimming a ruddy long way. Doing the Channel?"

"Last night I was on a picket-boat," I gasped.

It was over twelve hours since I'd spoken to a living man, and my voice was almost gone. "A waterlogged boat, it was. There were about twenty of us."

"Did they have any stores on?"

"No, nothing."

"Same here," he said. "Sorry I've no dry socks you can put on, Royal!"

"That's all right, Chiefie," I said. "I shan't get chilblains."

"That you won't, any road. Lucky to have your bloody toes."

There were, as I say, about fifty of us aboard my first night on the Carley, but whether we were fifty alive, or with only a margin of warmth and life left in our bodies, I could not tell. As the Northern Lights flashed around us and we knew another night was closing in, we discussed among ourselves the chances of being picked up.

"How d'you know they sent radio signals before the Abandon Ship?" asked a matelot pugnaciously.

"I tell you they did," said the Signal Bo'sun calmly. "I saw the signal being sent."

"Well, it hasn't done any ruddy good, has it?" argued the matelot.

"But it might. There's time."

How much time? The optimists among us said maybe twelve hours.

I judged it was about midnight when the first man died. Still I was not sleeping. Sleep eluded me. But I was gazing at the Northern Lights when there was a hell of a rumpus behind me, and one man was hammering blows on the face of his companion and shouting: "I'm telling you, you bugger. I'm telling you. I'm not taking any more of your lip."

By the time we pinned his arms back, he'd half smashed the other man's face in.

"Cut it out," said the bo'sun. "We've enough trouble without you. Cut it out."

"But he was giving me his lip," said the man. "I stood enough on the gun, but I'm buggered if I'll take that sort of talk from him."

The bo'sun touched the eyelids of the injured man, then turned away.

"You're crazy," was all he said. "He didn't give you any lip. He's been gone an hour or more."

And the other began to whimper like a child. "Staring at me, he was, and going on at me like a mad thing."

"You're crazy," said the bo'sun.

Under the flickering Northern Lights I gazed around at the men who were left. One was singing softly to himself. A rating pilot, he was, still with his orange Mae West over his shoulders, the remains of his P.O. naval rig suit in tatters. There was something about his voice.

> "*Smile the earth, and smile the waters,*
> *Smile the cloudless skies above us,*
> *But I lose the way of smiling…*"

He sang on, so softly he meant nobody else to hear. But that voice. A chord echoed in my memory.

"Know a bloke called Johnnie?" I said.

He looked up, blank for a moment, then said: "Yeah, Johnnie. I know him. Pal of yours?"

"No," I said. "But I'm trying to place you. Isn't your name Dogget, or Locket, or something like that?"

"Beckett," he said. And then: "Well, for Pete's sake. You're the Marine who scared the guts out of a girl in the dockyard. You Royals do get in some funny places."

8

"IT wasn't that way at all," I said.

"What the hell do I care how it was?" he said. "It was dark, and you were there, and the girl was there, and I said to myself 'Lucky perisher.' Well, I was just joining the *Glorious* on what might be a long tour of duty, and I kind of felt lonely having just kissed good-bye to my own folks, you follow. So you made me envious."

"It wasn't that way at all," I said. "It was just a girl from the pub at the top of the harbour there..."

"Oh, that sort."

"For God's sake, stow it," I shouted.

"I'm sorry," he said, and we fell silent for a long time. In the next hour or so we hardly exchanged a word, but mutely we thumped each other to keep the circulation going.

Several times we scrambled down the raft when there was a call for help or a whimper as a man died from exposure, and we tried to pass the bodies over the side. But after a while we hadn't the strength, so we could do nothing but watch them die and let their bodies rest at the bottom of the float. Being a Carley, we were almost knee-deep in the sea.

"You know," I said to Beckett some time next dawn, "it wasn't that way at all. About that girl in the dockyard, I mean..."

"Oh, for Christ's sake," he said.

"No, I'd like to tell you, if you don't mind."

He shook his head and smiled wanly. "I guess there's not many others to listen, if you feel like talking." So I told him. The words were jumbled, and I don't know if he really understood. But I felt better for the telling. I told him how it wasn't my girl, that the last time my girl and I embraced was over two and a half years ago; and that it was a damn silly song running through my mind which took me back in memory, and I felt I was kissing Peg.

"I know how it is. Two and a half years is murder," he said. "It does things to a man."

"You blokes are lucky. You don't get long commissions like that."

"We have now, chum."

Beckett was a navigational type, and I talked to him about my Gulf Stream theory; that maybe we'd drift near land, even if it was Greenland. Possible, he agreed, but in my heart I felt it was just a lot of talk. Anyway, thank Heaven we could talk. My secret fear was that our tongues, so swollen in our salt-scarred mouths, would swell to such a size we should choke to death. So I kept on talking to any of the lads who'd listen, to make sure the tongue was in my head and could move.

I'd be talking in a whisper, but just loud enough to keep my tongue and lips on the move, and the chap next to me would grunt or spew; but it was all so clear, so near to me. I got angry when I couldn't make them understand.

Those runs ashore. Tony's Bar in Malta, where you got steak, egg and chips for one-and-three... the Au Bon Goût in Alex, where with every bottle of beer you ordered they served up those little dishes of potato chips, cheese straws and savoury meat rolls, so you went on ordering more beer… I could see all this in clear, blue-shadow reality. Why couldn't these idiots see it, too? Why not? They were there, too. Suddenly I realised I was talking to Beckett.

"Cut it out, lad," he was saying, as though in answer to my thoughts. "I was never out East."

"You should have been," I said. "It was a good time for you pilots."

And then another picture came into my mind. "But maybe not," I said. "Maybe not."

"Why?" he asked. "What went wrong?"

"It was the night-flying exercise," I said. "That's the night I don't ever want to see again. All night long we were flying off aircraft on the exercise. I got a few hours' sleep up near the flight-deck, but I was bunked near a square open port and I could see them take off in threes… one straight off from the flight-deck, one port, one starboard. Then they did a roll like Prince of Wales' feathers. And every time one came on there was the god-almighty clatter of the arrester wires, then they'd be up again in another Prince of Wales' feathers.

"I lay down to get some kip, and there was one hell of an explosion, and when I jumped to my feet the sea was on fire. Two of the blokes had collided, coming out of a roll.

"The sea blazed right away to the horizon, but one of our escorting destroyers went through the wall of flame and picked up the injured. We went as close as we could, and lowered a boat. There were four dead, and the others couldn't speak for weeks.

"We buried the bodies wrapped in sailmaker's cloth, and put up a launching-platform on the quarterdeck. It was the first burial at sea I'd ever seen…"

"I've never seen death before this," said Beckett softly. "It takes some getting used to, to my way of thinking." Then, suddenly, almost suspiciously: "How is it I never saw you before?"

"You did. With the tart. Remember?"

"No, I mean in the *Glorious*."

"I didn't mess with the W.O.s," I said. "I was a flunk. One of the cushiest jobs in the Service."

"Good for you," he said. "Well, better look after the living than the dead. That's what I always say…"

I followed his gaze. One of the chaps with a bit of strength left was scrambling round the float, heaving bodies over the side. But, in a sort of frenzy, he clawed at the pockets and belts first, stuffing notes, silver and photographs into his own belt.

I gave Beckett a look.

"What the hell can we do?" he grunted. "The perisher's crazed. If we stop him, there'll be a scramble. No, tell you what, Tubby. We'll give him a hand. Let's get the jerseys and jackets off the bodies. It's a waste of clothing that might help to keep the others warm."

So we started on this ghoulish job, with hands beginning to swell unrecognisably with the extreme cold. The sweaters and jackets we handed round, and all shared.

Then came a terrifying moment. The crazed fool scrounging the money off the bodies began to mumble and moan, blubbering wildly to himself. He took out a roll of notes from the belt and rubbed them in his hands, crying like a child.

Then without warning he rose and faced the fore part of the Carley and ran with almost superhuman strength and speed, with a laugh that echoed as he leaped.

He sank and drifted by us; the pound and ten-shilling notes he had collected fluttering around. Then, pulped and soggy, they drifted and sank away, too.

For some queer reason, I did not talk to any of the chaps about the hunger and thirst now so terrifyingly urgent. Nor did I even give vent to the thought that unless we could get something fresh to moisten the tongue and lips, they would swell to choking point.

It must have been a peculiar form of conceit that made us, individually, very loath to talk of things as they affected *us*, but ready and anxious to help those who were already dying from the want of the things which tortured us, too.

Secretly we tried all the devices of Nature to relieve thirst.

I would not let even Beckett see me leaning down to the bottom of the raft and moistening my lips with the salt water; and though my eyes burned like fire with scanning the horizon for hope of rescue, I did not let him see that the periodic flushing with the salt water was becoming more frequent, that I could not resist this temptation even though the salt was beginning to cut into the flesh like acid.

I didn't tell him. But, privately, I knew he was doing just the same.

The second night the Northern Lights were not so bright, and away in the gloom at the other end of the raft I could hear two men talking. I nudged Beckett, at my side, and together we listened.

"If those sods try to come it, use the knife," one was croaking.

"The one with the Mae West won't come it. He's almost had his chips," whispered the other.

"But that Tubby. He's the sod. He's the one that got all the jerseys off them. There's plenty of spunk left in him. He's the one to watch."

So we went on listening. And when they moved, scrambling round the float among the bodies lying there, eyes wide open like fish, we kept still — knowing that to start a fight now in our weak state would only hasten death. My nerves trembled, though my swollen limbs were now too frozen to move. So we watched.

Pray God I may never see it again. These two demented men were nibbling at the fingers of the dead, trying to get blood to drink.

Beckett half lifted me by the arm.

"Boy, this is it," he whispered. "I thought it was a crazy dream, but now I see those bastards are really doing it."

"They're mad," I mumbled.

"It's a risk we've got to take."

They never had a chance, because they were stooping over the dead when we fell on them and blindly struck out with our last remaining strength. They grunted, then fell silent along by the bodies they were crazily mutilating. And Beckett and I lay with them for a time, because we were now too weak to stand.

"The crazy maniacs," I breathed. "If we've got to go, at least let's go decent."

"I reckon they didn't know," he said. "That's what I want to think anyway. They just didn't know."

It was fortunate that we lay there and slowly regained a little of our strength, for early on the fourth morning Beckett and I saw the last remaining shipmate go demented. I never knew his name, but I'd know his voice and his screaming face as he lashed into me while I hung there to the ratlines trying to ward off his blows. Then, choking, he toppled over and fell into the black water.

"You Marines are pretty tough," gulped Beckett with an attempt at a laugh that ended as a croak.

"You're not doing so badly yourself."

"But you saw all the others in that picket-boat die."

"Yes."

"You're not bloody well going to see me die."

"That's the stuff, birdman," I said. And then, when I'd worked out my own idea of the answer, I asked: "What day do you think it is?"

"The way I've worked it out, this is the fourth day since you came to the raft. What d'you reckon?"

"That's what I make it," I said. "I've cut notches in the canvas here each time the Northern Lights faded, and I've counted that a day."

"Four days. Four bloody days. Do you think you can stand another?"

"I can stand anything I know. What's beginning to worry me, watching the way the others go, is that I'll fall asleep and go crazed, and not know when the end comes. Will you promise me something, chum?"

"If I can do it."

"You can do it," I said. "If I go crazy, just cut me loose. Don't give me a chance to play merry hell if I don't know what I'm doing."

"For God's sake," he said, "don't you go nuts. You're a lot bigger than I am. I don't want to start handling a ruddy crazy giant."

"Okay," I said. "Okay, I was only asking."

The day wore on, and I felt too weak to continue carving the little criss-cross pattern on a bit of driftwood that somehow we had picked up in the Carley. So I sat there and nodded, and tried to shield my eyes from the salt glare, and as I did so a sudden warmth enfused my body, and my ugly, swollen arms became supple. Supple enough to feel.

We were rocking, then I realised it was not my movement but the instinctive swaying of her thighs as she slipped out of his grasp, then looked back and laughed with that high-pitched laugh. And, watching them flirt together, I joined in the laughter, and the girl whose face was all lit up, with the smiling eyes, was watching, too. And we touched hands.

"Don't call me a scouser," she said. "It's an ugly word, and I don't like ugly things."

"They were ugly times," I said. "Pretty ugly, back in the 'twenties when things were bad and there was only lentil scouse in the pot at home. That's what my dad used to say."

"Aye that I did," Dad cut in. "It was worst about the time Walter and you were kids. I was all right, of course, because I settled down in the boot business when I came out of the Army in 'eighteen. But it was cruel hard on the others who hadn't got jobs. And cruel hard on the women."

"Forget it," said the girl. "It'll never be like that again." And she went on singing, and we all joined in, and the song became a dance, and I was rocking with happiness, my whole frame shaking with the joy, my cheeks stinging with the warmth and the joy of it all…

Beckett was shaking me like a rabbit, and punching first one stinging cheek, then the other.

"Snap out of it. For Pete's sake, snap out of it."

"Wha' — what'm I doing?" I mumbled.

"You were dozing, man. You were singing. We don't want another crazy perisher in the float. That's why I had to punch you in the guts to make you wake up."

"That'sh all right," I mumbled drunkenly. "What — what was I shinging?"

"Some Jock song it sounded like. Something about the rose and the heather."

123

"Oh, that one," I said. "Yes, I know." And it went on round and round in my head, humming and buzzing. The humming note grew louder, until at last I realised it was not only a sound from the note of memory but the throb of an engine. It was, for certain, the drone of an aircraft. One of the Walrus coastal craft so familiar in the *Glorious*.

"God, d'you see that?" I called to Beckett. "Wave, man. Shout. Yell your bloody head off. We've got to make them hear us."

And he rose like an oily, dishevelled scarecrow, and together we clasped arms so we wouldn't stumble, and we moved and screeched until we were hoarse, our parched lips cracked and bleeding.

9

THE Walrus banked away and in a few seconds was lost to sight. Beckett and I stood clutching each other's arms, staring red-eyed after it, too heavy-hearted to speak.

I turned away and nestled slowly down in my place by the edge of the Carley, and Beckett sank to the framework, letting his hands run in the icy water. His shoulders heaved. He was crying, great silent tears.

An hour or more afterwards we heard the drone again, and what might have been another Walrus passed over. We didn't get up and wave. There was an awful fear in my heart. I didn't believe the aircraft was there.

"D'you see that?" I called to Beckett.

"Yes, I saw it."

"Then it was real!"

"I don't know, I don't know," he said dejectedly.

"But if we both saw it...?"

"It was on your mind as well as mine. Oh hell, what's the use...?"

"Know what I want, more than anything?" I said suddenly. "A good kip. I haven't dared go to sleep until now. Now I don't care any longer."

"Dangerous to kip," said Beckett. "You won't wake up."

"Depends how long. Look, if we take it in turns... One of us'll sleep while the other keeps watch, and then after an hour or so..."

"All right."

He flung himself down and I clutched him like a woman, and we pressed our bodies together to keep in what little heat we had.

"Don't worry," I said. "I'll wake you."

I let him sleep for maybe a couple of hours, but he woke without my having to punch him.

"God, it's cold," he whispered. I'd let him sleep too long. In that temperature I realised such lengthy inaction would still the blood in our veins for ever. We had a pummelling match, then I had a cat-nap. And so we kept on.

I was nursing him and gripping him together when my grip grew strong with amazement, and I saw what seemed to be the spurt of smoke on the horizon. A ship! A German ship?

Then I released my grip, and let the sleeping form fall into my lap. It was no ship but the spouting of a whale.

The whales were spouting all that morning. I reckon our Carley had startled them. Well, thank God; if we had to go into the drink at least there'd be a quick finish, and we wouldn't just float around and rot.

I was gazing at the whale spouts, Beckett's oily form pressed to my naked breast, when I saw a spout that didn't die down again to the sea's surface like a devilish fountain. It was wispy and indeterminate, on the horizon. I sat up and peered hard. There was no doubt about it.

Smoke!

I punched him awake, and together we watched the plume develop into a funnel, then the masts came, and it was a small trawler.

We started to wave.

"They can't see us. We're too low in the water."

"Hang on," yelled Beckett. "I'll wave my Mae West. They'll see that."

I held his legs while he scrambled on to the edge of the Carley, and stood poised there draping the soaking yellow lifebelt.

For one horrible moment I thought he was going to stumble, and I was almost too weak to hold him like that. In our struggle the Mae West slipped from his grasp, but I managed to drag him back into the Carley, then lean over and grab the rubber cloth before it slid away like a streak of gold into the green.

We stood back to back, and with our last remaining strength we waved the Mae West like a flag, higher and higher...

She seemed to continue on her course as if she had not seen us, but it was only the peculiar optical effect of looking out to the horizon, and our brine-closed eyes could hardly see. All colour, all feeling was fading. I only knew the trawler was near when the great black wall of her hull cut out the feeble Arctic light, and a rope ladder was hanging from the side. I groped towards it like a blind man, and so did Beckett.

"*Hurtig*! *Hurtig*! *Vaer forsiktig...*" shouted the blue-jerseyed figure leaning over the gunwale.

"Oh, Christ," I thought. "It's the Jerries." But now it didn't seem to matter any more.

Strong arms gripped and steadied us and helped us up the ladder, and I passed out at the top of it. To be Nazi prisoners after all we'd been through was more than I could stand.

When I came to, I was lying on the deck in the warmth of a galley fire. A sailor passed me a cracked enamel mug with some hot spirits in it, and I pushed it aside angrily.

"I don't drink with any blamed Nazis!" I spat.

"*Nazis? Nazis?*" He had a laugh like it came from a deep cavern. "*Vaers god...* This Norge... Norsk..."

"Norwegian! Norwegian!" I shouted.

His great frame rocked again with laughter.

"*Ja! Gô pâ!*" And he mimicked me. "Norrr-*veeg'n!*"

Then I stretched my arm out. "Now I'll have that bloody can of hot rum!" I said.

Some hours later I awoke to find myself crammed in a bunk with a chap whose matted, greasy hair half hid a familiar face. He was a stoker from the *Glorious*. In other bunks — there were four altogether — and on the deck lying wrapped like cocoons in rugs and clothing were about a dozen more survivors.

In God's name, why was I among this small but fantastically lucky group of survivors? All told, there were only less than three score out of nearly 2,000, and as the months rolled on I was, in fact, to discover that some of those saved were to die in hospital from their injuries and from exposure.

But now, at this precious moment I was safe. Why? *Why?* At the time I could find no answer, and in stumbling words I kept thanking my Creator. Then I began to get sick of being told: "You were a lucky sod, Tubby!" And I searched back in memory for an explanation. After all, there must be a factual explanation, even if you call it an act of God.

Now, I'm not trying to cast blame on individuals, on naval equipment or regulations, but I think these are the outstanding reasons why I had a better chance of survival than some of my mates.

I was fat. Fat is the best protection against Arctic cold. Some of the lads were bogged down with wollen "comforts" which froze their limbs. I was half naked, but fat.

I was lucky, too, in not being exposed to serious shock or burn during the action. Although I did my stint at the G.P., it is probable that I escaped some blast and burns of the shelling when I went with that party to see what we could do about the hangar fire. Some of the men — hundreds, perhaps — must have died at once from shock on jumping in, because already they were in need of attention for critical shock or more than third-degree burns. I was just lucky.

Why had I survived in the boat, when all the others died? Because I was tougher? Maybe. Because I was not shocked or injured? Maybe. But I think the handful of glucose sweets somebody shoved into my hand ten minutes before Abandon Ship probably helped to save my life. I'd gobbled most by the time I jumped. The others in the boat may have had no sugar or anything of a vitamin nature for several hours, and in that extremity of human endurance this tiny factor could be the dividing line between life and death. There were no supplies in the boat. Of course, there should have been. But there weren't.

A third reason why I fared better than the others in the boat was that the men had roped themselves in tightly, and I protested to the Surgeon-Lieutenant when they expected me to do so. They believed they were doing the safe thing. But to my way of thinking — and it is only a personal point of view — they would have fatigued themselves far less if there had been more slack in the rope, so that as waves drove over the boat they would have had rope-space in which to move.

Why was I, along with Beckett, lucky in the Carley, when all the others died? Now, for Beckett the answer is simple. He did not join the *Glorious* until Greenock, he had not been with us out to the Middle and Far East and so his blood was not thinned. But why did *I* survive? I do not think fat is the only answer. Submersion in salt water seems to have something to do with it. A Carley float, you must remember, is not a raft. It does not have a platform which floats *on* the water, but in it. Only the huge, cylindrical outer shell of the Carley floats on the water, and the central platform goes about three feet down in the water in either direction, depending upon which face of the Carley hits the water when the float is launched.

Most people would think it better to be in a dry lifeboat than knee-deep in a Carley; but in some magical way

Nature's affinity with salt seems to preserve life, provided you can withstand the extreme cold of the Arctic, and that's where being fat helped. It's the way my Maker made me.

But, of course, now I was suffering from the exposure, and at first in the trawler I did not realise how serious this was. I only knew I could not walk. Even to crawl was agony.

As my strength came back, I dragged myself from the bedfellow warmth of the stoker and crawled out on deck. It must have been four or five hours later.

"*Vent her!*" called one of the sailors, motioning me to get under cover, and I listened as he did. And above the roar of the waves heard the drone of a twin-engined bomber.

"That's a Dornier!" I said. The drone became a roar.

"*Ja, Dornier,*" he agreed, "*Jeg har hodepine.*" And he banged his forehead as if he had a headache.

"It does more than that to me, matelot," I said. "It turns my guts over."

The roar became a drone again, and we could hear the Dornier circling for about five minutes. Then it flew off, the pilot obviously going back to bomb up.

Twenty minutes later we ran into fog. I hate the fog at sea, but this time we thanked God for it. It was crazy, being scared of the sound of an aircraft after what we had been through, but now the danger was over I no longer felt keyed up, my resistance was cracking and even the little things hurt.

We ought to have been grateful to those Norwegians for what they did for us, and at heart we were. But we were a difficult lot. We drank all their fresh water in twenty-four hours; then asked for more, so they had to distil some in the engine-room. We groused at the iron taste of that, but lapped it greedily. They needed the fresh water, too, to make soup for us, as few of us could take any solid food. We lay in our bunks cursing the whole blamed thing, and for a change we struggled out on deck and cursed the slowness with which we were reaching land.

And all the time those damn wonderful Norwegians just slapped us on the back with their: "*Det gjør ikke noe.*" And I got to know what that means soon enough. It means "san fairy ann."

By this time I had a chance to know what was happening to my hands and feet. They were terribly swollen and dead white. There were large blisters, too, apparently from the extreme coldness of the water, but oddly enough these didn't pain so much. It was the numbness of my legs and arms that grated night and day, and though I slept at first through sheer weakness, as strength returned I lost the ability to sleep, and my mind kept travelling the same path of horror all over again, ever since the first salvo struck the flight-deck of the *Glorious*.

Each day we kept asking our rescuers when we should reach home or land of any sort, and always the reply was: "*Imorgen.*" At first I thought that meant "In the morning." Then I found it meant "Tomorrow." It seemed like a hundred tomorrows before we saw the grey line of land, then the green above the rocks. And it was the Faroe Islands.

On board came a Major and his staff of the Lovat Scouts, a Scottish Regiment stationed in the Faroes at the time. And Christ, was it good to hear English again? Even with a Lovat accent?

They examined us as we lay there in our bunks in the trawler, and after sorting us out they transferred us to the ready-waiting ambulances at the quayside. Some of the lads were able to walk with the aid of a soldier at each arm, others, like me, had to go on stretchers to the ambulance. Some went to the army camp. I went with a batch to the Danish hospital at Tórshavn. They figured we were the worst cases, which wasn't very encouraging.

They stripped me naked and left me in a cradle stretcher. And then a girl in a white overall came in with a tray containing a wad of wool and a bowl of spirit. I tried to cover myself with my great white swollen hands, like bladders of lard, but she only laughed and said: "*Nevn det ikke...*" I supposed I looked Norwegian, in the raw.

"I don't know what you said, Miss," I said, "and you don't know what I'm saying either. But I'm funny about things like that, and that's why I'm keeping my hands on my you-know-what."

"And if you know what's good for you," she said in almost perfect English, "you'll keep your great silly hands by your sides. I've got to wash off the oil with surgical spirit!"

What happened after that wasn't so funny. As she painted and scraped the oil off the brine-soaked skin, she discovered a wound which I didn't know was there.

She looked at it and could not conceal an anxious expression. Then the doctor came and had a look, and being a good doctor he didn't let me see he was anxious, too.

"It's black, isn't it?" I said. "That's gangrene, isn't it, doc?"

He shook his head and said nothing. The white-coated nurse stood silent, too.

"Look, Miss," I insisted, "if it's gangrene I've a right to know."

Without batting an eyelid she said: "The doctor's sorry, but he doesn't speak any English."

"Then what's the word for gangrene in your lingo?" I asked, but they both went out quickly.

She came back soon and got busy at that wound again. When it was cleaned and chipped away it looked better, and after a lot of muttering between the nurse and the doctor, and when they had taken a test on an oil-soaked bit of dead flesh around the wound, he came back and heartily thumped me on the back, saying with a Scots accent you could cut with a knife: "Ye'll be a'right the noo. It wus naw but a bitty oil!"

"Well, for Jesus' sake!" I gasped. "When I'm fit and on my feet again, I'll give that nurse what for!"

But I never did. Suddenly we got word that destroyers were being sent to the Faroes to pick up all survivors, and within forty-eight hours of landing we were again on stretchers and being carted by ambulance to the jetty, where the destroyer *Veteran* was waiting. The good Danish folk gave us a complete outfit, with underclothes, and flannel trousers which had to be split up the legs to pass over our bandaged feet.

On the *Veteran* they treated us like ruddy heroes, but I felt ill and my legs were getting worse. The last stage of the journey seemed never-ending, though in fact it took only two days to Port Edgar, near the Forth Bridge.

There were some chaps walking on deck, and I turned to see a familiar face, still sun-tanned despite the ordeal. It was Hill — Lieut.-Commander Hill. I could have cried.

"I've only just heard you were aboard, Healiss," he said, and he seemed genuinely pleased to see me, happy to know that all we shared on the *Glorious* was not quite lost.

We talked about the others. Names. Faces. People. Very real people to us, but now only a handful were still living out of nearly two thousand.

"There's — there's nothing much we can do at the moment, I'm afraid," he said.

"Do?" I asked blankly.

"Well, I mean… we can't have a drink for old times' sake or anything like that, can we?"

"No, sir, we can't," I said. "Not while I'm on this confounded stretcher."

"Well," he said, rising to leave with an awkward urgency. "Have a pint on me when you get settled." And so saying, he slipped two pound notes into my stretcher.

After Port Edgar, they took us to the Royal Naval Auxiliary Hospital at Kingseat, where I settled down to hospital routine with a cradle over the feet so I could not see the chaps in the beds opposite, but could natter only with the survivors to left and right.

By now the news had reached home, delayed as there was no wireless on the Norwegian trawler. Peg and my family had received the first grim news from the Admiralty: *"Missing. Presumed killed in action."* Now they knew we were safe, but at first for security reasons could not be told where.

"Hell," I moaned. "It would be some dump right up in Aberdeen, so that even if Peg knew she couldn't get here."

Unknown to me, the Padre had sent a wire.

I heard footsteps in the corridor, familiar footsteps I had not heard for nearly three years, but which I recognised before the white doors swung open.

I closed my eyes and heard the lilt of that friendly voice. Then soft fingers rested on my bandaged head, and warm lips caressed my cheeks. Peg was by my bedside, and that was the comfort I'd prayed for. I was home, wasn't I?

Appendix

THE OFFICIAL RECORDS

Admiralty Communiques on the Loss of the Glorious:

Communique No. 16: Information of contact between our forces and German forces in northern waters.

Communique No. 17: *Glorious.* Must be presumed lost. Captain G. D'Oyly Hughes, D.S.O., D.S.C., R.N.

Communique No. 23 (18th June 1940): Some survivors landed in this country.

THE NAZI VIEW

(The following is an English transcript of an eyewitness account of the sinking of the *Glorious*, as broadcast on Nazi radio, 12th December 1940.)

"I had the exciting experience of being on board a warship far out in the North Sea, near Trondheim, when the British aircraft-carrier *Glorious* was sent to her doom.

"This was the first time the warship had come face to face with a fully-equipped aircraft-carrier. An aircraft-carrier possesses a powerful attacking weapon which at the same time can become its most effective defence — that is, aircraft. The *Glorious* had fifty on board, also comparatively strong medium artillery, torpedoes and A.A. batteries.

"Her strongest protection against naval forces consisted of her high speed — 32 sea miles an hour. She was also safeguarded by two British destroyers escorting her, both of which had heavy torpedo armament.

"The most dangerous weapon was put out of action without effective warning, and in fact all heavy artillery had already fired *before our adversary had recognised us as being the enemy*. Their 'flying death' was reduced to ruins.

"As the engines were going at top speed, our heavy artillery was keeping the aircraft-carrier under fire. The medium artillery warded off the destroyers which tried to withdraw the carrier from the range of our destructive power, partly by enveloping it in a smoke-screen, and partly by trying to keep off our warships or by luring them away by bold but futile attacks.

"The result was that our heavy artillery destroyed the aircraft-carrier, *in spite of the most desperate defence of their medium artillery*. And it was despatched to the regions of Father Neptune."

WHY THE "GLORIOUS" WAS THERE

The following official extracts from the Admiralty's *The War at Sea* explain the tactical reasons for *Glorious* being exposed to attack in northern waters.

Vol. I:

The first phase of the war at sea, marked by the opening submarine campaign, was over by the end of October 1940. Convoys had started and were running. The second phase of the war was largely concerned with raiders. The first report came of one on October 3, when survivors of the British S.S. *Clement*, landing in Brazil, reported their ship had been sunk (about 75 miles S.E. of Pernambuco) by a surface raider. This proved to be the *Admiral Graf Spee*.

It became known later that three raiders had been at work, two in the North (*Scharnhorst* and *Gneisenau*), and one (*Graf Spee*) in the South Atlantic.[1]

The blockade was being enforced at that time by the light cruisers of the C and D classes, and armed merchant cruisers in the northern patrol. To meet the ocean raiders, a number of groups were constituted as follows:

FORCE F: *Berwick*, *York*. Disposition: North America and West Indies.

FORCE G: TWO of *Cumberland*, *Exeter*, *Ajax* or *Achilles*. Disposition: East of South America.

FORCE H: *Sussex* and *Shropshire*. Disposition: South Africa, West.

FORCE I: *Cornwall*, *Dorsetshire*, *Eagle*. Disposition: Colombo, Ceylon.

FORCE J: *Malaya*, *Glorious*, *Ramillies* and Australian destroyers. Disposition: Aden area.

FORCE K: *Ark Royal*, *Renown*. Disposition: Freetown, Africa West.

FORCE L: *Furious*, *Repulse*. Disposition: Atlantic Convoys.

FORCE M: *Kent* and *Suffren*. Disposition: Sumatra.

CONVOY DUTY (North Atlantic): *Revenge*, *Resolution*, *Warspite*, *Emerald*, *Effingham*.

---

[1] *Graf Spee*: 10,000 tons. Six 11-in. and eight 5.9-in. guns. 26 knots. *Scharnhorst* and *Gneisenau*: 26,000 tons. Nine 11-in. and twelve 5.9-in. guns. 27 knots.

When it became clear that for the military operations to succeed, fighter support was essential, the aircraft-carriers *Ark Royal* and *Glorious*, which had just returned from overseas, were placed under the orders of the C.-in-C., Home Fleet, and left Scapa for Norway on 23rd April, arriving next day.

The Skuas and Swordfish from the *Ark Royal* and *Glorious* did splendidly useful work, and on 25th April were 90 miles inland protecting British troops, while thirty-three aircraft in an attack on Trondheim (25th April) destroyed three hangars and a number of aircraft. A further raid was made on Trondheim on 27th April. This arduous work in fog and snow brought a signal from the Admiralty: "We are proud of the Fleet Air Arm."

It was in fact the first time in history that carrier-borne aircraft had been employed in prolonged operations of this nature, and the Fleet Air Arm aircraft were under the disadvantage of being outclassed by the shore-based aircraft opposed to them.

After a brief respite at Scapa and the Clyde to make good aircraft losses, the *Glorious* and the *Ark Royal* were ordered to the Narvik area on 30th April.

The *Ark Royal* fighters afforded protection there from 7th May until R.A.F. landing-grounds were ready towards the end of that month. The *Glorious* and also the *Furious* embarked squadrons of Hurricanes and Gladiators, and left for Narvik on 14th May. Both the *Ark Royal* and the *Glorious* were employed at Narvik during the final evacuation of Norway in June, the former providing fighter protection, the *Glorious* evacuating R.A.F. fighters.

On 8th June, *Glorious*, which had been sent to Narvik chiefly to evacuate the R.A.F. fighters, was sunk by the German battleships *Scharnhorst* and *Gneisenau*, as well as the attendant destroyers *Acasta* and *Ardent* and the merchant ships *Oil Pioneer* and *Orama*, with the anti-submarine trawler *Juniper*.

No enemy report was received from any of these ships.

It was not until 0938 hours on 9th June that the C.-in-C. Home Fleet received a report from H.M.S. *Valiant* that she had met the hospital ship *Atlantis* which had seen an attack on the *Orama* at 0900 hours on 8th June, in 67.44 N., 03.52 E.

Dispositions then made by the C.-in-C. proved too late to be effective, and extensive air reconnaissance over the whole of the North Sea at dusk on the 9th revealed no sign of the enemy.

Some thirty-seven survivors picked up by a Norwegian ship reached the Faroes on 13th June, and from their accounts it was learned that the enemy opened fire at 1600 hours on the 8th on the *Glorious* at 20,000 yards. She was hit by the third salvo which prevented her aircraft from flying off, and destroyed the bridge and the wireless. She was outranged throughout, and sank at 1730 hours.

The destroyers attacked with torpedoes, but both were sunk. The *Oil Pioneer* and *Orama* were not in the company of the *Glorious* and destroyers, but were proceeding independently. No ship in the Narvik convoy had previously been lost.

SUBSEQUENT HISTORY OF THE "SCHARNHORST" AND "GNEISENAU"

After the action on 8th June 1940, it was reported that one of the destroyers succeeded in torpedoing the *Scharnhorst*. Both the *Scharnhorst* and the *Gneisenau* were attacked during the historic R.A.F. bombing of Brest. *Scharnhorst* was not hit at Brest, it is recorded, but was bombed on several occasions during her cruise of La Pallice.

At Brest, however, the *Gneisenau* was struck by an R.A.F. bomb which did not explode, and the Nazis could not at once ascertain if it was a time bomb or a dud. They hastily undocked the ship preparatory to dealing with the bomb. An R.A.F. torpedo aircraft attacked her almost at once after leaving harbour, and she had to return to dock.

While in Kiel, another R.A.F. raid occurred, and the *Gneisenau* was hit on a magazine vent shaft. Cordite charges began to go off one after another, and she was burned out. The *Gneisenau* was laid up at Gdynia, and took no further part in naval operations.

A complete description of the *Scharnhorst* and *Gneisenau* in the closing phrases of their operational life is given in the *Sunday Times*, 24th June 1945, to which the reader is referred.

POLITICAL BATTLES ON FATE OF THE "GLORIOUS"

The loss of the *Glorious* in such tragic circumstances, and the fate of so many men from the carrier and attendant destroyers resulted in Parliamentary questions over a period of several years. The reader who is anxious to study the political implications of the loss of the *Glorious* is directed to *Hansard*, Vol. 365, No. 123, 7th November 1940.

In addition, the following *Hansard* quotations show the nature of the political implications as they developed in subsequent years.

Mr. Stokes asked the First Lord of the Admiralty whether he will now make available to the public the report on the inquiry held on the loss of H.M.S. *Glorious*.

Mr. Brendan Bracken: No, sir. The reports of Boards of Inquiry are confidential and are never published.

Mr. Stokes asked the Parliamentary Secretary to the Admiralty if he will give the names of the ships forming the normal escort to H.M.S. *Glorious*, three of which were not with her at the time she was destroyed by enemy action.

Mr. Dugdale: There is no question of any particular ships, or a particular number of ships, ever having been allotted as a normal escort for H.M.S. *Glorious*.

Mr. Stokes asked the Parliamentary Secretary if he has any further statement. Is it not a fact that the proper escort, the cruiser and two other destroyers, were taken away from the *Glorious*. If it is also not a fact that neither the officer commanding Coastal Command, the officer commanding Submarines, nor, I think, the officer commanding Home Fleet, were told of the movements of the *Glorious*, and in consequence thousands of men were left rocking about in the water, and nobody went to look for them.

Mr. Dugdale: I cannot possibly accept that statement.

Mr. Stokes: Well, it is true.

Mr. Medland: Will my Hon. Friend say whether any orders were received direct from the Ministry of Defence, over and above the Admiralty, to divert destroyers away from these men?

Mr. Dugdale: I am afraid I could not say that without notice.

Mr. Stokes: Well, it is true.

Mr. Stokes asked the First Lord of the Admiralty whether he is aware that before the sinking of the *Glorious* it was laid down by his department that no aircraft-carrier should go to sea without an escort of a light cruiser and four destroyers…

Mr. Dugdale: Detailed instructions of this nature are not issued by the Admiralty… The Navy at that time was stretched almost to breaking-point. Besides the tremendous task of guarding all our trade routes, the evacuation of Boulogne was actually in progress, and preparations were being made for the evacuation of Dunkirk, which was carried out only three days later.

THE LOSS OF THE *GLORIOUS* MUST THEREFORE BE SEEN NOT AS AN ISOLATED TRAGEDY, BUT AS PART OF THE SACRIFICE THAT HAD TO BE MADE DURING THE GREAT OPERATION OF BRINGING BACK OUR EXPEDITIONARY FORCES IN PREPARATION FOR THE DEFENCE OF OUR OWN SHORES.

A Note from the Estate

Ronald Healiss was born in West Derby suburb of Liverpool on 23rd April 1914. As a young boy he was a strong swimmer and spent many hours teaching younger children how to swim, little did he know just how useful these skills would be later in life.

After school he became an apprentice Chef with British Railways Hotels, starting at the Adelphi, Liverpool before spending time in Birmingham and Glen Eagles in Scotland, specialising in butchery. Before the outbreak of the Second World War he decided that he would join the military. He first applied to the Scots Guards, but was rejected because he was two inches too short of the six foot requirement height, before being accepted into the Royal Marines in 1933.

Plymouth was his home port and it was while based at Eastney barracks in Southsea that he met his future wife. HMS *Glorious* was part of the Mediterranean fleet and he spent the later 1930s travelling to places such as Malta, Gibraltar, Alexandria, the Red Sea and Ceylon. Shortly after the outbreak of the war HMS *Glorious* was brought back to British waters and based in Scarpa Flow to support the retreat from Norway, which is why it was in Arctic waters when set upon by the *Scharnhorst* and *Gneisenau*.

After being demobilised in 1946 he looked for jobs as a cook, but struggling to find anything in this line of work he found employment in one of the many manufacturing companies in area as a Commissionaire, which gave him the opportunity to join the Corps of Commissionaires due to long military service. He rose to become Chief Commissionaire at

Skefko Ball Bearing Co. Ltd. and was a trusted, personal assistant to the Directors and Senior Management of the SKF Group.

Although he managed to record his memories in *Arctic Rescue* he rarely talked about his experiences and could never be found on Remembrance Sunday while other members of the family watched the commemoration at the Cenotaph on television. One of his saddest times was the cessation of his meagre disability pension from the War Office soon after the publication of his book and would wonder whether he had raised too many questions over the tragedy of HMS *Glorious* and the huge numbers of lives that were lost.

In 1979 he retired but sadly passed away on Christmas Day the following year at the age of sixty-six. He was warned by Naval Surgeons in Scotland after rescue in the Arctic that *if* he survived the effects of the extreme frostbite, then if he reached age 50 he would have the body of a man of 80!

Thank you for reading, we hope that you enjoyed his book and if you have enjoyed it enough to leave a review on Amazon and Goodreads, then we would be truly grateful.

The Estate of Ronald Healiss

Sapere Books is an exciting new publisher of brilliant fiction and popular history.

To find out more about our latest releases and our monthly bargain books visit our website:
saperebooks.com

Printed in Great Britain
by Amazon

36482547R00088